# THE JAPANESE

# HOW THEY LIVE AND WORK

*Volumes in the series:*

# The Japanese

## HOW THEY LIVE AND WORK

W. Scott Morton

PRAEGER PUBLISHERS
New York · Washington

BOOKS THAT MATTER

Published in the United States of America in 1973
by Praeger Publishers, Inc.
111 Fourth Avenue, New York, N.Y. 10003

Library of Congress Catalog Card Number: 72–93298

Printed in Great Britain

# *Contents*

# List of Illustrations

*(The photographs not otherwise acknowledged are included with the kind permission of Japan Air Lines)*

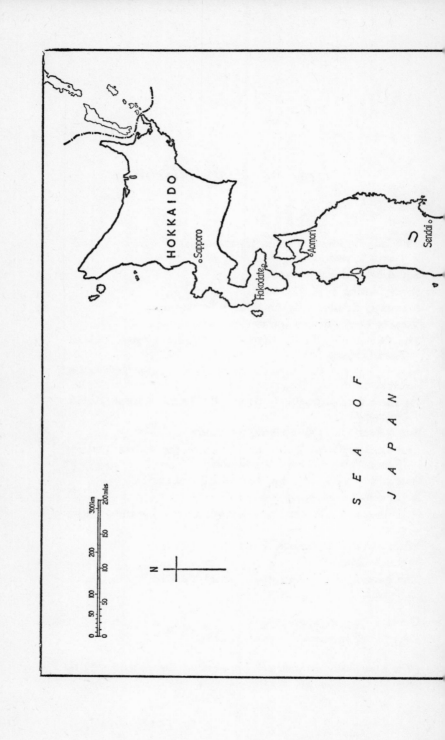

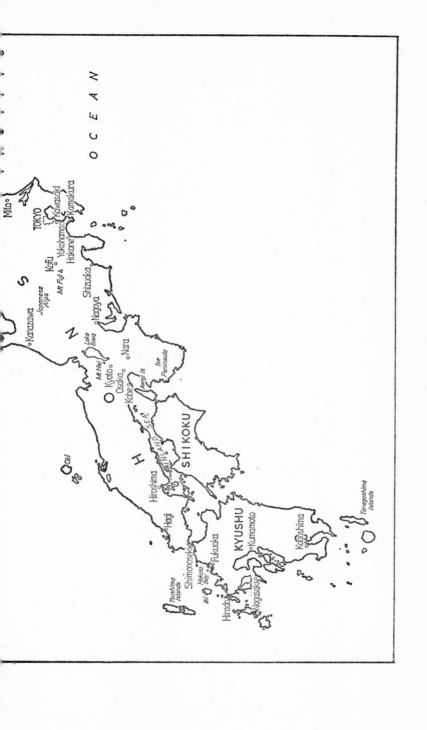

# Introduction

THE constant test for anyone attempting to write about the people of another nation is to imagine, as he writes, his words being read by the nationals of the country he is presuming to discuss. That the Japanese are a proud and sensitive people makes the task in this instance perhaps more than usually delicate; but in that the Japanese are also realists, the prospect becomes a little less formidable. The facts need only be put down; they speak for themselves, for Japan's modern performance is one of the most remarkable phenomena of our age.

The Japanese historically have excelled in two capacities, contradictory to us but quite compatible in their own view: as warriors and as artists. In their first capacity we in the West at first admired them and then were repelled. In their second capacity, we also admired them but found them exotic and 'quaint'. The determination and drive which made them fighters have also made them extremely successful in the economic world. Their true artistry has a universal appeal; but they themselves wish that we would graduate to a view of Japan which is beyond the quaint, the adolescent 'Madame Butterfly' image. It is to bring to the average man in the West a more straightforward and down-to-earth view of the Japanese today that this book has been written. Within its appointed limits it can only be a vignette.

The contrasts between old and new Japan are very great and not a little intriguing. Many brief references to traditional Japan are made in what follows, for the newest of the new Japan

always has its roots in the nation's past. Japan has been successful beyond anyone's dreams in modernisation; yet it has not
been without cost. When Commodore Perry landed in 1853
to establish relations between Japan and the United States,
many Japanese soldiers were still using bows and arrows, and
it is said that Japan then was at about the stage of development
reached by Tudor England 400 years before. To condense into
100 years the progress made by the West over 500 years is remarkable, but the process has been accompanied by a certain
psychological stress. This psychological stress was compounded
by the fact that the defeat suffered by Japan in World War II
was the first defeat in her history which resulted in an invasion
of her soil, in other words total defeat.

Japan has recovered. She still has problems, connected with
internal politics (including corruption), international trade relations, defence, housing, pollution and a deep malaise and uncertainty among many of her youth. But what nation has not
these problems?

To see how the Japanese run their country and conduct their
lives is interesting, and may be instructive. The study of Asia
by the West, and especially the study of the great giant, China,
and the little giant, Japan, is really no longer optional for us;
it is compulsory, if we are to live in the modern world.

# I

# *The Country and the People*

## THE LAND—PHYSICAL CHARACTERISTICS

JAPAN is an island country where the ocean is never very far away. The tree-clad promontories jutting into the Inland Sea form secluded bays above whose shore-line lie terraced fields of emerald green rice-plants, and old thatched farmhouses surrounded by clumps of feathery bamboo. Islands and even tiny rocks crowned with pine-trees are dotted over the distant level stretches of the sea.

Inland there are sharp contrasts, craggy mountain ranges rising to 12,000ft, volcanoes venting smoke, sulphur fumes and sometimes lava, snow-slopes for skiing, and even glaciers in the Japanese Alps. From the deep winter snows and summer pastures of Hokkaido in the north, Japan stretches through almost sixteen degrees of latitude to the semi-tropical regions of Kyushu in the south-west where palm-trees and oranges flourish.

Japan consists of four main islands, Hokkaido, Honshu ('mainland'), Shikoku and Kyushu, and thousands of smaller islands, and forms a land area of 145,670 square miles, approximately the size of California, and just over one and a half times the size of the United Kingdom. The south-west end of Japan lies some 120 miles off the tip of Korea and 540 miles east of Shanghai. The northernmost point of Japan is 500 miles east-north-east of Vladivostok. If one were to superimpose the map of Japan upon that of Europe, placing the northern tip of Hokkaido over the north of Denmark, the south-west end of Kyushu would fall somewhere between Barcelona and Madrid.

13

Now transfer the map of Japan to the east coast of the United States, the north part on the Canadian border. The south-west would then reach in a long sickle-curve to the northern edge of Florida and west into Louisiana. Honshu, the principal island, is very much larger than any of the other three main islands, so much so that in the European comparison it alone would stretch 875 miles from Amsterdam to Florence, and in the American one from New York City to Atlanta, Georgia.

Underneath the scenic beauty of Japan, however, there lies a constant underground threat. The islands are perched on the edge of the great Pacific trench known as the Tuscarora Deep and are liable to strains and shifts in the earth's surface which produce thousands of earthquakes each year. The majority of these are minor, but the earthquake and consequent fire of 1923, which lasted for three days and destroyed all of Yokohama and half of Tokyo, took the lives of 100,000 people.

Rainfall varies widely because of topography but most of Japan has a precipitation of over 40in a year (considerably more than that of the nearby continental north China). The vegetation is therefore lush and beautiful. The short and fast-flowing rivers descending steeply from the mountain ranges are useless for navigation, but valuable for hydro-electric power production. The life of the people from time immemorial has been determined by the surrounding sea. Some of the earliest archaeological evidence of human life in Japan is provided by mounds of sea-shells thrown out by the primitive inhabitants. Even today the major amount of protein in the Japanese diet comes from sea-food, fish of all kinds, shell-fish, octopus, squid and shrimp. Seaweed is used both as a vegetable and an appetiser.

As to sea-borne trade, Japan may be considered well situated by her geographical position. Internal exchange of goods has long been carried on more easily and profitably by sea than by land. External trade with the Asian continent, especially Korea and China, was possible even in ancient times, since the distance from south Japan to the end of Korea is only 120 miles. Yet this narrow sea-barrier was sufficient to protect Japan from marauding enemies, while still allowing fruitful cultural contacts from the mainland civilisation to reach her.

In respect of her island fortress position off the coast of a great continent, Japan is somewhat similar to Great Britain. Both have benefited by the proximity of other countries and other ideas, and yet been able to maintain their own independence and to develop their distinctive ways of life. Both have in modern times maintained successful navies manned by men to whom, as fishermen and coastal traders, the sea was a friend, or at least a familiar enemy. Japan, poor in natural resources and with only 17 per cent of her land arable, has had to depend as much as Great Britain upon the skilled manufacture and export of goods to supply her people with the necessities of life.

## THE PEOPLE

The people of Japan belong to the Mongolian family of mankind, which includes the Chinese and Koreans as well as the peoples of the Mongolian steppe lands. The Japanese, almost without exception, have the black hair, dark eyes, yellow skin pigmentation, high cheekbones, comparatively flat plane of the face and eyelid-fold distinctive of this race of mankind. In smaller stature and more delicate bone-structure they resemble the southern Chinese rather than their nearer north China neighbours. Their exact racial origins are obscure. One strain in the early mixture which gave rise to the Japanese of historic times seems to have come from Siberia and Mongolia over the Korean land-bridge, another strain from south China and possibly by a long sea-route.

By temperament the Japanese have a natural enjoyment of life; by circumstances and necessity they have become extremely industrious; and through their history they have developed a sense of loyalty and national solidarity second to none. Some would say they combine the qualities of warriors and artists. As fighters they have courage, stoicism and a streak of cruelty; as artists they have an unusual sensitivity to the beauties of Nature and an ability to use with simplicity and unerring taste the natural substances of stone, wood and clay.

In addition to the Japanese there are still a few pure Ainu tribespeople living on reservations in the northern part of the country. These are descendants of early inhabitants of Caucasian origin whose totem is the bear, who live by fishing and hunting, and who were once widespread over the country but were conquered by the Japanese. Another minority group is that of the *eta*. These people were in earlier Japan a servant-class who performed tasks such as the slaughter of animals and the tanning of leather considered unclean in Buddhist belief. Although they now enjoy complete equality under the law, there is still some social discrimination against those of *eta* origin, especially in regard to marriage.

## POPULATION

The population of Japan in March 1970 was 103,522,000. This places Japan seventh in the world, after Mainland China, India, the Soviet Union, the United States, Indonesia and Pakistan, in that order. Regular census figures began to be taken in 1721, when a population of 30 million was reported. This figure remained fairly stable during the rest of the Tokugawa Period, but after the introduction of modern industrial processes it began increasing and rose from 34·8 million in 1872 to 98·3 million in 1965, thus multiplying 2·8 times in just over 90 years. The rate of increase has declined markedly since World War II from 2·5 per cent per annum in 1948 to 0·7 per cent in 1965. The average family size in Japan today is 2·5 children. During this same period, 1948–65, the density per square kilometer rose from 217 to 266. In present density of population, 278 persons per square kilometer at last count in 1969, Japan is fifth, after the Netherlands, Taiwan, Belgium and South Korea, in that order. The seriousness of the problem of overcrowding in Japan is shown by the fact that 70 per cent of the people live in cities, and of that urban population no less than 58 per cent are located in only three metropolitan areas, namely Tokyo, Osaka and Nagoya. This makes the historic 400 mile stretch of the Tokaido (East Sea Road) between the seventeenth-century military capital, Edo (or Tokyo), and the ancient capital of Kyoto practically one long megalopolis today. The population of Tokyo has passed 11 million, giving it the doubtful benefit of being the largest city in the world. Osaka has almost 3 million people, Yokohama (near Tokyo) and Nagoya each over 2 million.

Immigration took place at nearly ten times the rate of emigration in 1950; but now the rate of each is balancing out at approximately the same numbers in and out per annum.

## HISTORICAL LANDMARKS

The Japanese emerge from the mists of pre-history about the time of Christ. By this time some of their leaders had left an early home on the island of Kyushu and set up a centre of power in the Kansai plain around the future Kyoto and Nara and extending down the Ise Peninsula. The people were organised in clans, led by a warrior élite, with special groups responsible for handicrafts, religious functions and agriculture. The successive leaders of the Yamato clan in the area just named seem to have had a special sacrosanctity and to have established, not without a struggle, a political dominance over the others. From this clan came the future emperors of Japan, which makes this by far the oldest ruling family upon earth. A profound change came over Japanese civilisation with the arrival of Confucian and Buddhist ideas from China and Korea in the sixth and seventh centuries. (The official date for the introduction of Buddhism is AD 552.) The use of a script borrowed from China made possible the keeping of accurate records and ultimately the rise of literature. The prestige and efficiency of Chinese methods of government led to the attempted establishment of a

B

bureaucracy in AD 645, which, however, never fully replaced the fundamentally aristocratic structure of Japanese society.

The eighth century saw a spectacular rise in Buddhism, the building of great temples and production of numerous images, some of surpassing beauty. The capital, after varying with the residence of each emperor, was first fixed at Nara in AD 710 and then at Kyoto in 794, where it was to remain until the move to Tokyo in 1868. By the tenth and eleventh centuries Japan was less culturally dependent on China and was producing a distinctive literature of her own. The chief example of this native literature is *The Tale of Genji* by a woman writer, one of the great novels of the world.

But life at the capital, under the brilliant leadership of the Fujiwara family who intermarried with the emperors, was becoming too isolated and precious. The focus shifted to the country estates and the military families. A series of conflicts culminated in the Gempei Wars between the Taira and Minamoto families, which ended in the victory of Minamoto Yoritomo and the setting up of the Kamakura Shogunate in 1192. Rule by a *shogun*, or chief general, on behalf of the titular emperor became a feature of the Japanese penchant for indirect rule from this time onwards. The military government, or *bakufu*, was centred first at Kamakura, then after 1333 at Kyoto under the Ashikaga family, and after 1600 at Edo (the modern Tokyo) under the Tokugawa, until it was abolished in 1868.

The first *bakufu* government of a feudal type was strong and efficient, and succeeded in defeating two serious invasion attempts by the Mongol dynasty of Kublai Khan. Under the Ashikaga central control became weaker. This, however, was also the golden age of Japanese art, which has set the standard for all subsequent aesthetics in Japan. This age felt the inspiration of Chinese Sung Dynasty painting, and saw the rise of the Nō classical drama and the peculiarly Japanese development of the religious-aesthetic tea-ceremony.

A period of destructive civil wars in the 15th and 16th centuries was gradually brought to a close by three of the greatest leaders in the history of the country, Oda Nobunaga, Toyotomi Hideyoshi and Tokugawa Ieyasu. In spite of rivalries each built upon the foundations of his predecessor's work to bring political stability to the country. It was during their time that Japan first had contact with the Western world. The Portuguese arrived in the 1540s, but the Japanese gradually became suspicious of Western motives and ultimately banned all Western traders and missionaries, except for a few merchants from Holland who were confined to a small area in Nagasaki in 1641. (See under Religion, p 25.)

At this point the Tokugawa Shogunate made an experiment in the hermetic sealing-off of a country as effective as any Iron or Bamboo Curtain of the present day. By instituting a police state and banning all foreign intercourse save a strictly controlled trade with the Chinese and Dutch, the Tokugawa kept Japan isolated for about 250 years until the end of their régime in 1868. At the same time they gave her a chance to develop cohesiveness, discipline and comparative economic prosperity. Governments of today might note, none the less, that the attempt at isolation was never completely successful. The Japanese were extremely curious, particularly about Western advances in applied science, in fields such as gunnery, tactics, geography, astronomy and medicine. They obtained books on these subjects smuggled into Japan by Dutch traders. The feudal system was undermined by the rise of a new merchant class. Underemployed samurai warriors mingled with the merchants in the pleasure quarters of Edo and Osaka. New styles of genre literature and art in the form of popular colour prints gave evidence of a type of life very different from the ideals of the military régime of the past. Finally the old isolation was broken open and change accelerated by the forced entry of foreign traders after the treaties secured by Commodore Perry of the United States in 1854.

Certain clans, notably the Choshu and Satsuma, who were technologically advanced but politically conservative, then succeeded in a major coup d'état in 1868, doing away with the Tokugawa régime and re-instating the Emperor Meiji in power. He was only to rule, however, by the advice of an oligarchy of men who started as ambitious young samurai and ended as the Genro or Elder Statesmen of the new Japan.

The date of the Meiji Restoration, 1868, has been so constantly referred to in the above historical synopsis that it will be evident it marks the definitive entry of Japan into the modern world, and that not by accident but by design. She soon made up for lost time. By a co-ordinated national effort almost unmatched anywhere in the world Japan established and updated her industry, constructed railways, factories and a merchant navy, translated Western books, set up an educational system, adopted some forms of Western dress and customs, promulgated modern laws and wrote a Constitution in the Prussian style of Bismarck. Not least she built an army and navy able to defeat China in 1895 and Russia in 1905.

Prince Ito and other authors of the Meiji Constitution of 1889 envisaged a very limited role for the Diet and the political parties; but these, aided by the Press, came to assume an increasingly important position until, after World War I, a liberal era set in. Then several factors, including the worldwide economic depression, favoured the rise of the militarists in Japan. An imperialist drive, which had begun in Korea before 1900 when imperialism was fashionable everywhere, reached a new stage with the creation of the puppet state of Manchukuo in 1932. With Manchukuo as a base the Japanese Army attacked north China in 1937, which was in effect the first round of World War II. The war spread to the whole of China, and was enlarged by the attacks on Pearl Harbour and Singapore in 1941. Japan was finally defeated and had her country occupied for the first time in her history in 1945. The occupation was remarkably well conducted and successful, and the Japanese began to realise that they had been led astray by their own military leaders.

A new constitutional monarchy along democratic lines was initiated in 1946, and Japan started on the road to recovery. The story of her corporate rise from rags to riches in the last two decades is well known. The gross national product rose from $1·3 thousand millions (= USA billion) in 1946 to $149 billion in 1968, and Japan is now the third-ranking power economically after the USA and the Soviet Union. Although she may be expected to take an increasingly independent line in foreign policy, she has definitely thrown in her lot with the non-Communist Western world.

## RELIGION

*Shinto*

The basic, indigenous religion of Japan is Shinto, which means 'the way of the gods'. Legends about these nature deities, notably the Sun Goddess, are bound up with the early history of the Japanese race, and form a background to all their thinking and particularly to their love of country.

Shinto has no founder, no moral commands and no revealed scriptures. The nearest equivalent to scriptures would be two early chronicles, written down in the eighth century, recording both Shinto legend and early history of the nation. The name Shinto is derived from Chinese and came later; the religion itself is so original to Japan that it did not require a name. Shinto is a form of nature-worship or animism, which ascribes sentient life to inanimate things and the powers of nature. To understand the associations of the word *kami*, the deities of Shinto, a person raised in the Judaeo-Christian tradition will need to leave out the ideas of exalted holiness and otherness associated with God, and turn to something simpler. The notion of divinity in *kami* is connected with anything remarkable or notable in Nature—an odd tree standing by itself, a specially mysterious cave, the fertile rice-fields, the sun and moon, a tall mountain, an impressive hero, or even a queer form of insect— almost anything which inspires the feeling of awe.

Japan has some of the most beautiful scenery in the world, with snow-capped mountains, rice-fields like green jewels, and pine-clad promontories running down into a blue sea sprinkled with islands. It is small wonder that this beauty produced in the early inhabitants a feeling of gratitude and awe akin to worship. The principal Shinto deity is Amaterasu, the Sun Goddess; her brother, Susa-no-o, is the God of Storm. Among the best-known legends of early Japan is one which appears to be a myth explaining an eclipse of the sun. The Sun Goddess, offended by the rude behaviour of her brother, took refuge in a cave and refused to come out. All the gods and men were in great distress at this disastrous happening. One of the goddesses performed an amusing dance on an upturned tub and all the audience broke into laughter. The Sun Goddess, with feminine curiosity, poked her head out of the cave and was persuaded to emerge, and everyone was happy once more.

The grandson of Amaterasu was supposed to have descended on to a mountain-top in Kyushu, while his great-grandson in turn, the Emperor Jimmu, was accounted the first human founder of the dynasty which still rules Japan. This single dynasty, claiming to date from 660 BC, but historically established by AD 300 if not sooner, is thus the oldest reigning family in the world to rule without a break, with the possible exception of the rulers of Ethiopia. The latter claim descent from the offspring of Solomon and the Queen of Sheba, which would place their origins before 900 BC. But the romance of these two famous monarchs must be considered doubtful as a historical fact. The Shah of Persia recently celebrated the 2,500th anniversary of his country; but here there is no question of one ruling family. The Japanese imperial family's claim to length of years on the throne thus seems undisputed.

Shinto ceremonies, emphasising ritual purity, are carried on at many shrines, form part of certain public occasions, such as dedications of new buildings and prayers for the growth of crops, and are observed, as they have been from time immemorial, in the imperial court at the new year and at the enthronement of a new emperor. During World War II Shinto ceremonies accompanied the funerals of soldiers who had died in battle. The chief Shinto shrine is at Ise on the Yamato peninsula, which was an early site of Japanese civilisation.

Although Shinto has primitive traits, it has survived as a religion owing to its association with the family of the emperors and its stimulus to patriotism. It was deliberately promoted as a state religion at the Meiji Restoration in 1868, and used as a powerful propaganda weapon by the military prior to and during World War II. In spite of a recession after the war, Shinto still remains active and forms a permanent element in all Japanese life, though it no longer receives any special privileges.

## Buddhism

The other great religion in Japan is Buddhism, which came to Japan through China and Korea in AD 552. The religion took its rise in India a thousand years earlier, where the historic Buddha was born. His experience of spiritual release and the conquest of suffering and desire through meditation had a wide appeal. Buddhism spread in one form to Ceylon, Burma and South-East Asia, and in another to Central Asia, China, Korea and Japan. Before reaching Japan it had become thoroughly acclimatised and somewhat altered by the practical Chinese. It was valued in Japan partly for its supposed magical qualities in protecting believers from sickness and evil. But it came accompanied by a profound philosophy, an impressive ritual and an art and literature of great power. It appealed on all these grounds to the Japanese and, after an uncertain start, soon became rooted in their tradition. Emperors and nobles vied with each other in founding temples and monasteries at Nara, then Kyoto and finally all over Japan. Whole mountain tops, such as Mt Hiei and Mt Koya, became covered with monasteries, shrines and large cemeteries where many of Japan's most famous heroes are buried.

The buildings of a typical large Buddhist temple, such as those to be seen at Nara, include a main hall for the principal image, built in the Chinese palace style, a great gate with guardian deities on either side to keep away evil, a library, a pagoda, a lecture hall, monks' quarters and often a great bronze bell with mellow tone. The Japanese craftsmen, learning from Chinese masters, created images of strength and beauty in wood and bronze, exhibiting in their faces a calm detachment from this world and at the same time a compassion for struggling mortals within it. Although the untutored peasant of traditional Japan could not understand the subtleties of Indian philosophy, he could see the lineaments of goodness in these magnificent eighth-century statues.

But Buddhist art was not limited to statues. The artistic sense of the Japanese responded to and in turn created the beauty of calligraphy in the scriptures, scroll paintings, rich brocade hangings, priestly robes and impressive architecture on a grand scale. (See also temple gardens, Chapter 3, pp 62–3.)

Various sects were introduced from China and some were elaborated in Japan, for Buddhist sects are as many and varied as those of Christianity. Some of these were distinguished for their learning, some for their dependence on secret formulae and special diagrams (*mandala*). Others, such as Jodo ('Pure Land') and Shinshu, the most numerous sect today, encouraged simple piety and devotion, saying that to be saved, it was sufficient to call upon the name of the Buddha in faith. The medieval Japanese founder of Shinshu, Shinran, was beloved for his concern for the common people, when he went on preaching tours to remote places with his message of Buddha's compassion.

The founder of the Nichiren sect, on the other hand, was a militant figure, who insisted on denouncing other beliefs and criticised the government for not suppressing them. When the Mongols attacked Japan in 1274 (see p 18) and the country was in danger, Nichiren claimed that he had foretold this as a just punishment for the government's failure to promote true Buddhism as he saw it.

The most distinctive form of Buddhist belief and the best known in the West is Zen. Zen stresses meditation and spiritual concentration in the attempt to reach a psychological breakthrough, a higher perception of the non-identity of the self and an overcoming of one's sense of division from the rest of the universe, or the Buddha-nature. If the meaning of this last statement is not immediately clear, the reader need not be surprised, for the Zen insight is strictly ineffable, inexpressible. It must be personally experienced. Certain means have been developed by the Zen masters to lead the aspirant to the threshold of this experience, such as sitting in meditation, using mental puzzles such as 'What is the sound of clapping with one hand?' or even employing physical blows or kicks to shock the mind into awareness. The simplicity of Zen, its non-dependence on scriptures, its mental concentration and heightened sensitivity, and its identification with the totality of life have caused this philosophy to have a profound influence on the Japanese arts.

Buddhists in Japan today are given as 83,290,000 in number out of a population of 103 million; but it should be understood that Buddhism and Shinto may both be believed and practised by the same persons according to the occasion, as for example in Shinto rites for a marriage and Buddhist rites for a funeral. Or a family may, without any sense of contradiction, go at midnight of the New Year to receive a light for their hearth at the sacred fire of the Shinto shrine, and go on to the Buddhist temple the same night for the ringing of the great bell which drives away the 108 evil passions.

*Christianity*

Roman Catholic Christianity, introduced by the Jesuit pioneer, St Francis Xavier, in 1549, flourished during the following period, sometimes known as 'the Christian Century', but then was ruthlessly suppressed. Very successful at first, the religion came under suspicion because of its connection with the Portuguese and Spaniards, who, in the manner of the time, combined the account books of trade and the flag of imperial conquest with their devotion to the Cross in many parts of the world. Christians in Japan were persecuted, some were crucified in Nagasaki, a stronghold of the faith, and the religion went underground. As Japan began to open up again, Roman Catholics returned and Protestant missionaries began work in 1859. There was considerable Christian activity in schools, hospitals and churches. One interesting development has been the rise of a No Church Movement, whose adherents seek to practise the Christian life without organising themselves into a church.

The present constitution guarantees freedom of religion, but separates the functions of Church and State.

*No religious organisation shall receive any privileges from the State, nor exercise any political authority. No person shall be compelled to take part in any religious act, celebration, rites or practice. The State and its organs shall refrain from religious education or any other religious activity.*

The number of Christians in present-day Japan is about 830,000, with Protestants slightly outnumbering Roman Catholics. The influence of Christianity is, however, probably greater than this small number of believers (less than 1 per cent of the population) would indicate, since many leaders in public life have been affected by the ideas of Christianity in education and social welfare, as well as in their general outlook on life.

*New Religions*

There is a certain hunger for religion in modern, materialist Japan. So numerous have been the new religions springing up in the wake of the defeat and disillusionment of World War II that one author wrote a book entitled *The Rush Hour of the Gods*. The adherents of these new, popular religions feel that their beliefs are more adapted to modern times than the tenets of Shinto and Buddhism, and more adapted to Japanese life than those of Christianity. Most of these religions come from among the people and were founded by persons in ordinary walks of life, several of them women. Tenrikyo ('the religion of the heavenly principle'), for instance, was founded by a housewife. This religion is modern, but not among those founded post-war, for it dates from the late nineteenth century. Generally Buddhist in background, it stresses simple and joyful service and cleanliness. Tenrikyo believers run spotlessly clean work camps, and as an act of service turn out in large numbers to clear the large area in front of the Emperor's palace in Tokyo of all litter. To Western eyes the stress on cleanliness may seem superficial; and yet we are coming to re-assess the value of a concern for ecology and for a spiritual sense of the stewardship of the natural environment. At a deeper level the notion of ritual purity extends a long way back into Japanese history. Shinto worshippers rinse their hands and mouths before approaching the shrine, and everyone who visits Japan remarks on the constant bathing and personal cleanliness of the people.

Among the new religions the most numerous and fastest-growing sect, claiming 16 million adherents, is Soka Gakkai ('value-creating society'), likewise founded by a layman, a schoolteacher, Tsunesaburo Makiguchi, in 1937. Its beliefs are based upon the militant and nationalistic Buddhist creed of Nichiren, who lived in the thirteenth century at the time of the successful resistance to Mongol invasions. This sect appeals to the small businessmen, many of whom were forced into bankruptcy by the post-war crisis and the subsequent growth of large firms. 'Achieve happiness now', say the proponents of Soka Gakkai. 'You can get anything you want if you perform the chants and believe in Buddha.' It also appeals to the rural poor forced to seek work in the cities—girls in domestic service, for example—who have no trade union or group to which they naturally belong. Soka Gakkai runs an immensely successful publishing business with a number of magazines of wide appeal. It has devoted funds to the building of a huge centre and sports stadium at the foot of Mt Fuji. It makes an appeal to mass sentiment by the promotion of sports, bands and paramilitary organisations. It has been accused of strong-arm methods to gain converts, both in Japan and abroad. On the other hand it has stressed moral and religious values, and its demand for cleaner politics and its provision of a sense of community and fresh hope have met with a wide response.

# 2

# *How the Country is Run*

DURING most of Japanese history the country was run in the name of the Emperor either by a small group of civilian councillors or by a strong military leader, who in turn had his entourage of advisers. In 1889 a modern constitution was promulgated, including a Diet or parliament; but much of the effective power still remained with an oligarchy of advisers to the Emperor. After World War II, on 3 May 1946, a constitutional monarchy was set up, in which the authority rests with the representatives of the people meeting in the Diet. The Emperor's duties are purely ceremonial and executive power is vested in the Cabinet, which is collectively responsible to the Diet, on the British model. The Diet consists of the House of Representatives with 486 members elected for a term of 4 years, and the House of Councillors with 250 members holding office for 6 years, but with half of their number being elected every 3 years.

There is universal adult suffrage in present-day Japan, all men and women of 20 and over being entitled to vote. Members of the House of Representatives come from 123 multi-member constituencies, each constituency returning from 3 to 5 members. The members of the House of Councillors are divided into two groups, 100 being elected from all over Japan in the National Constituency, the remaining 150 from the 46 prefectures.

## THE CABINET

The Cabinet consists of the Prime Minister and not more than 18 State Ministers. The Prime Minister is chosen by the Diet and must himself be a Diet member. He appoints and dismisses the State Ministers, all of whom must be civilians and a majority of whom must be members of the Diet. The Cabinet takes collective responsibility for decisions, but rarely decides by vote. Matters are discussed until a consensus is arrived at, in the traditional Japanese way. Any member dissenting would normally resign or expect to be dismissed.

In the executive branch thirteen ministries are responsible to the Cabinet for running the affairs of government, namely the Ministries of:
Justice
Foreign Affairs
Finance
Education
Health and Welfare
Agriculture and Forestry
International Trade and Industry
Transport
Posts and Telecommunications
Labour
Construction
Home Affairs
and finally the Prime Minister's Office, which has under its wing no less than seven special agencies, which by their titles give clues to certain special emphases in Japan's aims. They are:
National Capital Region Development Commission
National Public Safety Commission
Administrative Management Agency
Hokkaido Development Agency
Defence Agency (for Self-Defence Forces, in lieu of Army, Navy and Air Force)

Economic Planning Agency
and Science and Technology Agency.


### THE JUDICIARY

The Judiciary is independent of the executive and legislative branches of the government, and consists of the Supreme Court (a Chief Justice and fourteen other Justices), eight high courts, prefectural district courts and various lower courts. The Justices of the Supreme Court are appointed by the Cabinet, but their continuation in office is subject to review by national referendum at the election following their appointment and again at ten-year intervals thereafter.

Before the war the administration of all courts was in the hands of the Ministry of Justice, itself a part of the executive branch of the government. Now Article 76 of the new 1947 Constitution places the 'whole judicial power' in the Supreme Court, giving it, on the American model, separate and equal status with the legislative and executive branches. The Supreme Court thus has three main functions, overseeing the administration of justice throughout the country, acting as a court of final appeal, and functioning as a court of judicial review. In this last aspect the Supreme Court has had little to do. There have only been two or three cases in which laws have been examined and held to be unconstitutional. The political function of a judicial body is simply not consonant with the Japanese understanding of the way to govern.


### LOCAL GOVERNMENT

Japan is divided into 46 prefectures, of which one is Metropolitan Tokyo, two more—Kyoto and Osaka—are urban prefectures, one—Hokkaido—is a large district, and the remaining forty-two are known as rural prefectures. They in turn are divided into cities (*shi*), towns (*cho* or *machi*) and villages (*son* or *mura*). There are 561 cities, 2,007 towns and 808 villages, a total of 3,422 administrative areas. Tokyo has self-governing districts or wards. Each city, town and village elects its own mayor and single-house assembly. The mayor selects his own staff, including the vice-mayor.

Government in Japan before 1947 was extremely centralised. Legally power lay in the hands of the Emperor and actually it was concentrated at the centre in Tokyo. Local governments had few rights and powers. Then with the post-war occupation came a complete about-turn. The aim was to make Japan a democracy and encourage political participation at the local level. Thorough decentralisation was to give local governments power and make them sensitive to local needs and demands. Hence the principle of local autonomy which was incorporated in Article 92 of the Constitution and the Local Autonomy Law which was enacted in April 1947.

All local governments are now semi-parliamentary, that is, the chief executive and the assembly depend upon each other. The executive can dissolve the assembly and the assembly can return a vote of no-confidence in him.

By law the local organs have wide powers of self-government; in practice they show limited initiative and a good deal of traditional dependence on the central government. This tendency is manifested in the following three ways. First, officials spend much of their time administering the policy of the national Ministries in the local situation. Second, the laws and regulations they put through are usually modelled closely on the sample legislation drawn up by Tokyo (see also under Education, p 88). And third, 20 per cent of their finance is derived from national subsidies or grants, which gives the central government considerable local control.

Such is the system of democratic government on paper; but one or two observations must be made upon its special character. First is the minor role assigned to the military, something entirely new in Japanese history. In Article 9 of the post-war Constitution Japan renounced for ever war as a means of settling international disputes. Minimal self-defence forces are maintained, numbering in 1970 just over ¼ million men, of whom only 38,000 were in the Maritime Self-Defense Force and 41,000 in the Air Self-Defense Force. Offensive armament in the form of large capital ships and long-range bombers or offensive missiles is entirely absent. Second—and this does not appear on the surface—decisions in Japanese affairs tend to be arrived at by consensus after consultation and compromise, and not by majority vote. The struggle for power can be as intense in Japan as anywhere else in the world, but in the course of the struggle the tendency is to avoid direct confrontation. Support is sought through the network of *giri*, duties and loyalties, which binds everyone in a complex system of mutual obligation. There are many signs, however, that today the traditional patterns of life are suffering erosion, and young people in particular are more independent in their thinking and action. This affects voting patterns, as does also the fact that the lower income-groups, both urban and rural, are better informed than ever before, and consequently less likely to vote as 'the boss' expects. Individual opinion seems to be slowly replacing older and more rigid configurations of society.

---

The Inland Sea, now shrouded in mist, now sparkling in sunlight, is famous in Japanese history and one of the most beautiful regions upon earth.

Most of Japan's protein comes from the sea. Here squid are being dried in the sun in the time-honoured way. The boats are typical small craft used for fishing in coastal waters around Japan.

## POLITICAL PARTIES

For almost the whole of the post-World War II period the majority in the Diet has been held by the conservatives in the now re-united *Liberal-Democratic Party*. The Liberal-Democrats support free enterprise, higher living standards, economic and social stability and general alignment with the policies of the West. This party is much the most powerful.

The opposition parties, reading ideologically from right to left, are:

*The Komei Party*, founded in 1964 as the political arm of the Soka Gakkai, a modern version of the Nichiren sect of Buddhism. This party advocates clean government, a form of welfare state and an autonomous foreign policy, not dependent on the US-Japan Security Treaty.

*The Democratic-Socialist Party*, formed after a 1959 split in the Socialist Party, looks to the bringing in of a socialist society through democratic processes and is against extremes in ideology. Among its policies are extended social welfare, full

---

Rice-planting in Hokkaido. The delicate shoots from the nursery plot are carried in bamboo baskets. They must be planted in standing water, a back-breaking job. Wide straw hats give protection from the sun. Light skin is a sign of beauty and sun-tan is something to be avoided.

A country family and a universal emotion. The Japanese dote on their children and spend freely on festival dress for them, as here. The tiered, thatched roof and tiled verandah roof are found in many farmhouses. Sliding screen-walls are of paper and glass in a wooden frame.

C

employment and the raising of living standards for the poor, along with an independent foreign policy.

*The Socialist Party* aims to achieve complete socialism in Japan through a peaceful revolution. It is opposed to the US-Japan Security Treaty and demands withdrawal of US military forces from Japan, and the provision of security through a four-power treaty including USA, USSR, Communist China and Japan.

*The Communist Party* presents the Communist platform in a manner designed to appeal to nationalist sentiment and particularly to youth and industrial workers. Since the time of the Cultural Revolution in China it has been anti-Maoist.

The standing of the parties in the House of Representatives after the last election in January 1970 was as follows:

| | |
|---|---|
| Liberal-Democrats | 300 seats |
| Socialists | 90 |
| Komei Party | 47 |
| Democratic Socialists | 32 |
| Communists | 14 |
| Independents | 3 |
| | 486 |

In this election the Liberal-Democrats gained 28 seats, the Komei Party 23 and the Communists 10, at the expense of both Socialist Parties.

In the various changes of government Prime Ministers have generally lasted longer than Cabinets, which have often been re-shuffled several times under one leader. From 1945 to 1965 the average term in office for a Prime Minister was 24 months (Ishibashi only 2 months, and Yoshida, a strong Prime Minister, 7 years), while the average duration of a Cabinet was 9½ months. During the period since the war there has only been one Socialist Prime Minister, Katayama, heading a Socialist-Conservative coalition for less than a year in 1947–8. All the rest have been Conservative. The last four Prime Ministers have held office for the following periods:

February 1957 to July 1960—Nobusuke Kishi
July 1960 to November 1964—Hayato Ikeda
November 1964 to July 1972—Eisaku Sato
July 1972 to present—Kakuei Tanaka

Those of more liberal and leftist tendencies find this situation very frustrating. Intellectuals and urban labour groups, unable to obtain a majority for their viewpoint in the Diet, have turned to confrontation politics and mass demonstrations. This has often made the surface of Japanese politics seem turbulent to the point of chaos, as when student-led riots in 1960 caused the cancellation of President Eisenhower's visit to Tokyo. But underneath, the election results showed a fairly steady conservative pattern, and the 'establishment' ruled with a firm hand.

### CURRENCY

Japanese currency is reckoned in yen (¥), with 100 of the smaller unit, sen, making one yen. But in practice the single yen itself is now so low in value that sen are never used. They may occur, but in certain book-keeping and investment quotations only. Yen are issued in the following denominations of bank-notes: 10,000, 5,000, 1,000 and 500, and as coins of 100, 50 and 10 yen value.

After recent fluctuations in the world money market, the yen has settled to a basic rate (May 1972) of ¥802 to the £1 and ¥308 to the US $1.

### TAXATION

National taxes in Japan have reached a level of ¥6 million million (£7,481 million, $19,480 million) a year. Local taxes are ¥250 thousand million (£312 million, $812 million). The national tax package is distributed approximately as follows:

1/5   redistributed to local governments
1/6   public works

1/7    social welfare
1/10   'other expenses' (there is no separate category for foreign aid, which falls within this group)
1/17   defence
1/30   education.

The percentage of income which is paid in taxes is roughly equivalent to the US federal tax rate. A Japanese college graduate working in the textile industry would earn about $2,700 a year, and pay 18 per cent or $486 of his income in national taxes.

### THE BUREAUCRACY

Before the war the Japanese bureaucrat, even down to the local policeman or postmaster, was regarded as the chosen servant of the divine Emperor, whose word was absolute law. The old saying *kanson mimpi* ('officials honoured, the people despised') was a good summary of the old-line bureaucrat's view of the public. The idea of a 'public servant' was nonexistent. Things are changing, but the vestiges of the old idea make it more appropriate to call the Japanese apparatus a bureaucracy than a civil service.

There has been a vast post-war expansion, from about 232,000 (less the military) in 1940 to about 1,632,000 government employees in 1965. A college graduate who has passed the appropriate civil service examination enters the sixth grade. Certain members of the three highest grades are extremely influential in the running of the country. This in-group of the higher bureaucracy normally number about 4,000 to 5,000 persons. Pre-war 92 per cent of this group were graduates of Tokyo Imperial University Law School and 4 per cent of Kyoto Imperial University Law School. Now there is a wider range of graduates from Kyoto, Waseda, Keio, Hitotsubashi, Nihon and other universities, but still the strongly entrenched Tokyo University clique tends to control admissions and promotions on the basis of old school loyalties. The Ministry of Internal Affairs used to be of most prestige for young aspirants but their hope now is to enter the Ministry of Finance, of International Trade and Industry or of Agriculture and Forestry.

Once a young man has survived the gruelling tests of examinations from primary school right through university and civil service entrance and has secured his place in a Ministry, his job is completely secure. But retirement comes early, about the age of fifty, and so he may soon be looking for a good position in industry. The necessity of ensuring provision for the future makes him vulnerable to favours and bribes in the form of jobs, gifts of stock, entertainment and so on. Japan is becoming increasingly an expense-account society. In 1964 alone, according to Robert E. Ward, the Board of Audit turned up over six hundred cases of misappropriation of public funds with a total value of seven and three-quarter million US dollars. Since the war more ex-civil servants are becoming directly involved in politics through running for election to public office after retirement. Their inside knowledge of government and bureaucratic process and 'connections' often enables them to render valuable and expeditious service, but has given them a prominence which is of doubtful value in the democratic process.

This is nothing new. There is a tradition from the days of the nineteenth century of bureaucrats becoming involved in politics. The tendency is strengthened at the present time by the fact that the Diet is not a very strong body and not very well suited to dealing with the complex problems of the modern world, especially in the international arena. Diet members often look to the experience and skill of bureaucrats, past and present, in matters of licences, public works, taxation, credit and bank rates.

### POLICE

Five men, appointed by the Prime Minister for five-year terms, stand at the head of a centralised police system in Japan. They are known as the National Public Safety Commission, and have as their executive the National Police Agency. The latter body co-ordinates the whole system and determines police standards and policies. The prefectural police forces have some autonomy on the local level, but in general conform to the national pattern, with little local initiative. The average local police station has about ten to twelve men, armed with pistol and short sword or dirk, the latter mainly symbolical. Women police have been in existence since 1946, but had only reached 380 in number by 1968. They are generally accepted by the force and are popular with the public.

Tokyo has a special Metropolitan Police Force, and five other cities, Osaka, Kobe, Kyoto, Nagoya and Yokohama, have municipal forces. The remainder of the country is covered by the prefectural forces, with the exception of Hokkaido, which, as a large frontier area only settled in the nineteenth century, forms a special case. There are approximately 24,000 policemen in all, one for every 4,300 citizens. Prefectures and the municipalities pay for their police services from taxes, but frequently have to apply for national funds to cover deficits.

Japan in the past was a highly paternalistic society, where the Emperor was the father of his people and anyone representing his authority, even at the level of the local official, was obeyed without question, save in rare cases of agrarian or industrial unrest. Individual rights have tended to be less important than community harmony. In these circumstances it may be readily imagined that the powers of the police were wide, and little restraint was exercised upon the activities of the dreaded secret police (kempeitai) under the military régime before and during World War II. The secret police were particularly tyrannical in Manchukuo and other parts of the Japanese Empire.

Things have changed since 1945. Police powers are now strictly limited, and the men are friendly and correct, though they still retain a strong sense of their own authority. They have every modern aid in their work, trucks, vans, cars, scooters, helmets, two-way radios—and Japanese thoroughness, discipline and efficiency. The delays of the law and the woodenness and rigidity of the petit fonctionnaire are doubtless also present here as everywhere in the world; but the impression conveyed by the Japanese police of today is generally very favourable.

The excellent organisation of the special force of riot police is of interest to many in Western countries who are concerned with the difficulties of controlling protests and demonstrations, now a world-wide problem. The morale of this special force is very high, and there is competition among policemen to enter its ranks in spite of the dangers involved. The riot police are organised in small, mobile units, specially trained to break up student demonstrations ('demos'). They carry shields and tear-gas equipment, and wear helmets and plastic visors. When attacked they will close ranks and cover their whole squad with a net to keep off larger missiles, and bide their time until they can move in with water-hoses or tear-gas, or until motorised reinforcements arrive. High morale is a large part of the key to their success, for they are much less liable to become provoked and magnify an incident by over-reacting than men who are not so confident or well trained. They have had great difficulties to contend with in the hit-and-run tactics, intelligent planning and determination of the large numbers of revolutionary students in Japan. The student mood, however, appears to be less militant now in the seventies than it was in the fifties and sixties.

## SOCIAL WELFARE

There are four types of social insurance which it is legally compulsory for an employer to provide for his workpeople. First is *health insurance*, in which the government meets the administrative cost and employer and employee contribute equal shares to the funds. In the case of the employee this amounts to 6 per cent of his monthly income. As benefit he receives medical treatment and 60 per cent of his pay for up to 6 months in case of disability, while his dependents receive half the cost of their medical treatment. For those not covered by an industrial firm's plan as above, a voluntary National Health Insurance scheme for the general public was established in 1938. Benefits, not so substantial as those in the above scheme, are obtained through contributions plus the proceeds of a local insurance tax.

The Japanese plan for health insurance thus seems to fall half-way between the private associations, such as Blue Cross in the USA, and the full compulsory national scheme as in Great Britain. These generalisations would have to be modified in detail, since, for instance, the USA now has for older persons Medicare and Medicaid supported by federal funds and compulsory contributions, and subjects Blue Cross to a measure of public control. The Japanese scheme combines government participation with coverage by private associations.

In the second type, *welfare pensions*, the state meets the administrative cost and contributes between 10 and 20 per cent of the benefits. Workers receive a pension on retirement, for which, however, they only qualify after 20 years of service. The National Pensions Law of 1959 provides a pension for any person not covered by another plan. Contributions are paid in to the scheme, and again 20 years is the minimum length of service needed to qualify. Widows and orphans, on the other hand, may qualify if the breadwinner has made three years' contributions.

Third is *unemployment insurance*. Here the state pays 33⅓ per cent of the benefit costs and all the administrative expenses. Workers qualify after six months' employment, and, while they are unemployed, receive 60 per cent of the average wage for the same kind of work as they were doing. They must, however, report twice a week to a centre and accept any job suited to their capacities, or enter a scheme for vocational training if required to do so.

The fourth type of protection, *workmen's compensation* for accident, requires little explanation. In this the employer has to accept all expenses of administration and benefits.

Public assistance is available to those below a minimum subsistence level, but a considerable social stigma is attached to accepting this aid. The procedures for applying are said to be humiliating and the benefits less than adequate. Thus more than half the eligible needy women and children do not even make application for assistance.

The Ministry of Welfare has eight bureaux, as follows: Public Sanitation, Medical Affairs, Pharmaceutical Affairs, Social Affairs, Children's Affairs, Insurance, Pensions, and Repatriation Assistance. Three per cent of the total government income is expended for social security and welfare programmes.

Japan is naturally not exempt from the common social problems. To name only two, suicides in 1963 numbered approximately 15,000; in 1965, 14,000. Though this represents a decrease, the suicide rate is still the highest in the world, and this is attributable in part to an ancient culture pattern. In Japan the incidence of suicide is greatest in the 15–24 age-group.

Secondly, prostitutes were said to number about half a million in licensed houses before the Anti-Prostitution Law of 1958. Since the passing of the law the numbers are no less and may be more. Now prostitutes solicit on the streets or act as call girls, hotel barmaids or masseuses.

(Source for the above figures on Social Welfare: *Area Handbook for Japan, 1969*, US Government Printing Office, prepared by the American University staff, Washington, DC.)

## DEMOCRACY AND DEVELOPING COUNTRIES— THE JAPANESE EXPERIENCE

There is concern at the present time over the best political road for developing countries to take. Should it be democracy at once? Or ever? Is democracy an exportable product? Should it be democracy of the Western style, or with some modifications to suit the ethos of Asia or Africa? And if the last, then what in practical terms does that mean?

Japan in the last one hundred years has gone through some profound changes which seem to have a bearing on this burning question. It is true that Japan's most crucial change took place in the nineteenth century, and must be described in terms no longer precisely current. For one thing Marxism was not as yet a major factor in world politics. But much of Japan's experience of political change is relevant and applicable to developing countries. The major turning-point from the old to the new ways, known as the Meiji Restoration of 1868, is therefore worth singling out, even in a short summary such as the present one, not only because it deeply affects the way the Japanese live and work today, but also because it has relevance to the rest of the world.

The new course was taken deliberately, after considerable doubt and debate. The events leading up to the change were marked by untidiness, inter-clan rivalry, strife and confusion. But once the main decision was taken to modernise the whole country in all phases of its life, no time was wasted and no effort spared to make the new policy work.

The policy itself was determined by both the future and the past. For the future, Japan had to have weapons to resist the West, for the alarming example of China's weakness since the Opium War of 1839 was not lost upon the Japanese leaders. These leaders, moreover, had the insight to see that the possession of modern weapons alone was no answer, unless the state had also the undergirding of a modern industrial system. This sub-structure of support for the armed forces could not be confined to the arms industry, but would have to extend throughout the entire economic network of the country. It would inevitably carry with it new ideas, but it was hoped that these could be limited and controlled. What the leaders had in mind was modernisation, not wholesale Westernisation, for they were passionately devoted to 'the Japanese spirit'.

It was here that the past was so strong a factor in the change taking place. The change was technologically bold to the point of being revolutionary; but politically and in spiritual outlook it was profoundly conservative. Japan had been familiar for centuries with a certain form of centralised state, with an emperor and his advisers, civil and military, in whom power was concentrated. The decisions of the nominal head, whether emperor or a general ruling in his name, were usually promulgated after consensus had been arrived at in a small group.

Much the same process continued to operate after the Meiji Restoration. The new ruling group consisted of a few court nobles, but for the most part of younger samurai from some of the most powerful clans who had opted early for reform. They intended to keep close control of the nation in the development period, and on the whole succeeded over the next twenty to thirty years. They have often been referred to as an oligarchy, but this is a Western term of reference carrying pejorative associations which—it will now be clear—it did not carry in Japan.

This inner group of men, later known as the Elder Statesmen, were, however, by no means static in their thinking. They had read well the Western lesson, and saw that democracy or republicanism—the sharing by the people in the process of government—was connected somehow with the remarkable growth of the Western countries in technology and power. Democracy seemed to work, and it seemed to be necessary as part of the whole modernisation package. Therefore Japan would have to have democracy. But let it be in a strictly circumscribed and manageable form. Let the Emperor not simply be retained but restored to his exalted position as the mystic centre of the nation and keystone of the social arch. The representatives of the people must only slowly be admitted to a partial share in the decision-making process, while the main work of government was being carried on by the Emperor's trusted advisers and the staff whom they selected to assist them.

In the early days of planning, one of the young samurai who had taken a leading part was Ito Hirobumi. He was destined to become the main author of the new Meiji Constitution, beginning his life on a small farm in the country and ending it with the title of Prince. His career was typical of several others in this time of transition who were influenced by a slightly older contemporary of theirs in the powerful Choshu clan, called Yoshida Shoin. Yoshida was a firebrand. He wanted to destroy the decadent leadership of the Shogun (generalissimo) and restore the Emperor to power. But to make Japan strong he saw that Western methods would have to be adopted. He tried to break out of the isolation of Japan by stowing away on board one of the ships of Commodore Perry in 1854, carrying paper and brushes to record the secrets of the Western nations. He was, of course, discovered and put on shore, only to be arrested. He spent a considerable time in house arrest, was later involved in a plot to assassinate one of the Shogun's officials, and was summarily executed in his thirtieth year. Visionary and impractical, he was nevertheless a born teacher, and while he was under house arrest in his home town of Hagi, conducted a small school which counted among its students Ito Hirobumi, Kido Koin, later to become Prime Minister, Yamagata Aritomo, father of the modern Japanese Army, and others. Exposure to Yoshida's heady new ideas and burning conviction decisively affected the lives of these young men and through them the history of Japan.

Ito Hirobumi, acting with more caution and foresight than his mentor, contrived to be sent by his clan to study in Great Britain, and returned to take a major part in the overthrow of the Shogunate and the restoration of the Emperor Meiji. He and his colleagues hastened slowly over the preparation of a Constitution. Ito went again to the West on a formal mission of research, but his mind was largely made up before he left. Although he visited Washington and London, it was in Berlin and Vienna that he spent most time, and Bismarck and the German political scientists who supplied the model for the new Japanese Constitution when it was finally promulgated in 1889. Ito and the majority of his collaborators felt that the paramount position of the Emperor could best be maintained with a political structure of the German type.

In summary it may be said that significant factors in the whole process of change, beginning in the 1860s, were: a coup d'état based on adequate military strength; consensus planning with some give and take; co-ordinated economic development, with government initiation of heavy industry, but based essentially on private enterprise; refusal to become dependent on foreign loans beyond a bare minimum; on the other hand extensive use of foreign technical experts and the rapid training of Japanese, who were then able to take over from the foreigners; and finally a gradual extension of the democratic process, in part planned by the leaders in the government, but in part unplanned.

The extension of democracy was the more remarkable because the Japanese were so far away from holding certain basic democratic ideas which seem self-evident to men in Europe and America. When a pioneer translator, Yukichi Fukuzawa, for instance, wanted to convey the notion of human rights, he had to invent a word since none existed in the Japanese language. His book, *An Encouragement of Learning*, caused a stir in the Japan of the 1870s because it began with the phrase: 'Heaven created no man above another, and no man below another'—which ran completely counter to the prevalent Confucian notion that society is a hierarchy of those above and those below, and that it is so because this is the pattern of the universe itself.

The Meiji 'oligarchs' had been able to hold the state together and to control Japan's development into a modern nation from the Restoration until the outbreak of World War I. By the end of the war most of them had disappeared from the scene, and effective power was distributed among various élite groups, such as the bureaucrats, the Privy Council, the military, the businessmen and the intellectuals. The use of power was therefore a matter of bargaining, and the medium of exchange, so to speak, for the bargaining became increasingly the political parties which rose to a place of importance in the 1920s. In spite of strife and scandals the machinery of party government gradually became a reality and the Diet was, more than before, a force to be reckoned with. This was the decade of Japanese liberalism.

In spite of every handicap democracy thus did take root in Japan owing to such factors as the power of the purse, namely ultimate fiscal control being vested in the Diet; the growth of newspapers, and hence of informed public opinion; the prestige of Western ideas, including Marxism among the intellectuals after World War I; the rise of political parties; and the self-generating increase of parliamentary participation, once the doors were opened, simply due to the fact that man is a political animal and political power is a normal human ambition.

Because the above outline is compressed, it gives an incorrect impression of neatness and unvarying success to the whole process. In actual fact the development of Japanese democracy was carried out in fits and starts. It was accompanied by political misjudgement, bribery, violence, assassination and all the undesirable factors which have been associated with active politics and emergent revolutions in every human society from Athens to Mexico City, not excluding London and Washington. But more and more the Japanese government has become responsive to the people's will. The present success of the Japanese nation, political as well as economic, which has become so evident in the post-World War II period, would not have been possible without the preparation in democracy, often underestimated, which took place between the Restoration and the military phase of the early 1930s. Although generalisations must be made with caution, it seems that in Japan democracy's long tutelage under 'oligarchy' worked because the Japanese were accustomed to discipline and community effort, and because they were fortunate at this crucial period in having as leaders statesmen of quite outstanding wisdom and courage.

After World War II an entirely new Constitution was drafted by the occupation authorities, modelled on the American system but with important elements drawn from Great Britain. The draft Constitution was discussed by the Japanese, was passed, and took effect in May 1947. The Preamble and Article I set forth clearly the sovereignty of the people and the position of the Emperor as a constitutional monarch.

*We, the Japanese people, acting through our duly elected representatives in the National Diet . . . do proclaim the sovereignty of the people's will and do ordain and establish this Constitution, founded upon the universal principle that government is a sacred trust, the authority for which is derived from the people, the powers of which are exercised by the representatives of the people, and the benefits of which are enjoyed by the people; and we reject and revoke all constitutions, laws, ordinances and rescripts in conflict herewith.*

Article IX renounced 'war as a sovereign right of the nation' or 'a means of settling disputes with other nations' and stated that 'land, sea and air forces will never be maintained' and 'the right of belligerency of the State will not be recognised'.

The Diet was made the only source of legislation, and the Cabinet was to be selected from the majority party in the Diet, as under the British system, and to be collectively responsible to the Diet. Other articles abolished the peerage, gave the vote to all men and women of twenty years of age and over, provided for a Supreme Court on the United States model, increased the powers of local self-government, and guaranteed not only freedom of person, domicile and religion, but also academic freedom and the right of collective bargaining.

Legally democracy in Japan had come of age. If there is a lesson for others, it is that of democracy by stages, under strong initial leadership and in a form suitable to the country concerned. But the Japanese were aware that a democratic Constitution on paper was one thing, making it work in practice quite another. When the first large delegation of Japanese went abroad again after the war in 1947, the Prime Minister reminded the members that delegations had been sent abroad after the Restoration to seek Western technology, but now the question was to find out how democracy worked in practice and what was its spiritual basis. These are questions by no means limited to Japan, but concern us all. The answers will have to be sought in co-operation.

# 3

# *How They Live*

THE traditional Japanese way of life has a self-consistent logic and beauty all its own. The distinctive note is economy and cleanliness, probably connected with the simple life and ritual purity seen in the early Shinto religion. The rooms in a Japanese house are uncluttered and scrupulously clean, and even quite poor people take baths daily. The national instinct for simplicity and good taste unfortunately often fails the Japanese when it comes to Western goods and furnishings. Only recently familiar with foreign imports, many Japanese tend to choose the tawdriest and most vulgar elements from what the West has to offer. The bulk of the population live in a style that is fundamentally Japanese, in Japanese rooms, eating Japanese food, but with the

---

The contrast between old and new Japan is nowhere better seen than in architecture. This revolving rooftop restaurant over the Hotel New Otani in Tokyo is centuries removed from the farmhouse on p 34. The nineteenth-century Diet Building (Parliament) is in the centre background.

The Ginza in Tokyo has become a world-famous fun and shopping street, with a cosmopolitan flavour. The name, given in earlier times, signifies, not inappropriately, the 'Silver Market' or banking quarter.

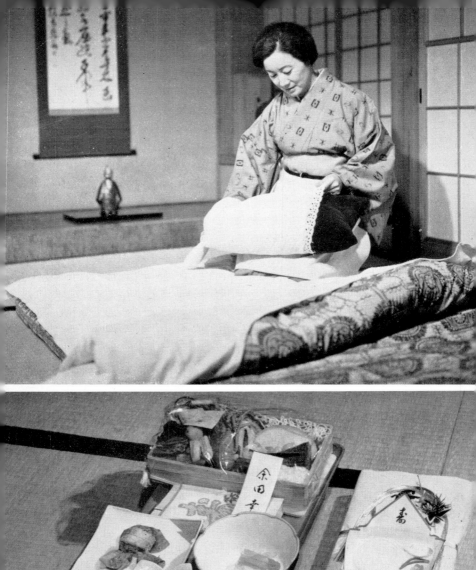

addition of Western gadgets and appliances, now manufactured in Japan.

### SHELTER

The Japanese are fond of colour, but this does not appear in their streets and houses except at times of festival. Traditional houses are low, one or two storeys, and built of unpainted wood or stucco with grey tile roofs, presenting from the outside rather a dull appearance. Gardens or features of decoration are reserved for the inhabitants and not displayed to the public gaze. Materials are simple and utilitarian, and full advantage has to be taken of the limited space available. So construction runs right to the building line on the edge of the narrow residential lanes, and the houses seem to face inwards rather than outwards. On commercial streets and main thoroughfares the number of rather untidy business signs and the presence of telephone poles and power-lines give a depressing air to towns and even villages. A few good modern buildings in the highly Westernised sections of Tokyo have a pleasant and sophisticated appearance at one end of the architectural scale. At the other end the more remote and unspoiled villages with thatch and weathered dark wood,

-----

Making up the bed in a Japanese room. The floor itself is a bed of padded straw-matting. Very closely woven, it has a natural straw polish and is easily kept clean. When the bedding is put away in cupboards, the room is used for eating and living during the day. The only decoration in these delightfully simple rooms is in the recessed tokonoma, where there is a picture and often an arrangement of flowers.

Japanese meals are served in dishes chosen by shape and hue to suit the food and appeal to the eye. Covers are used to keep rice and soup hot. Top centre, a tasty box-lunch. Bottom left, disposable pine-wood chopsticks in a wrapping, with the name of the inn or restaurant.

D

fronted by the sea or surrounded by pines, bamboo or green paddy-fields, are delightful. But there is a distressing amount in between, cities and towns which are uninspired, half Eastern, half Western, with the worst features of both, crowded, competitive, drab and higgledy-piggledy.

The Japanese themselves are the first to admit the unsightliness of urban sprawl. Amid their many sparkling successes in creating a new country and preserving much of the old, the more thoughtful of them deplore the shortcomings of modern Japan in housing, town-planning, drainage and environmental protection.

The greeting on arriving at a house, 'Please enter', takes the form, 'Please come up' (*O agari kudasai*), because the floor level of the house is above that of the entrance. You can take off your outdoor shoes in the *genkan* or stone entrance hall, and step up in your stockinged feet to the wooden verandah, and from thence on to the mat surface of the room proper. The standard *tatami* are 6ft by 3ft (Japanese measure, a little smaller than Western feet), and are about 4in thick, firm but with a little 'give'. The surface is a shiny one of closely woven straw. All Japanese room sizes are quoted by the number of mats, $4\frac{1}{2}$, 6, 10 and so on. Upon these mats the whole life of the household takes place, eating, sleeping, conversing or working. The rooms are thus economically designed as multi-purpose living spaces. They are enclosed by movable screens known as *shoji*, sliding in grooves in the floor and ceiling and covered with translucent paper. The screens forming the outside walls of the house may be partly glazed. The paper has some insulating properties, but Japanese houses are cold in winter. In summer they can be conveniently opened up for air. Rooms can be quickly merged into larger units just by removing the screens between them.

The most distinctive part of a Japanese room is the *tokonoma*, an alcove in one wall. It is furnished with a scroll painting, a vase of flowers and some shelves, often irregular in shape and supported by a tree-branch or other natural piece of timber. This focal point of the room formerly had a religious use as a small shrine, but the religious has now merged into an aesthetic sig-

nificance. The transition was easy to make, for in fact the realms
of the religious and the aesthetic are very close to one another
in Japanese thought.

Heating used to be entrusted to charcoal-burning *hibachi*, or
open stoves, placed in special square depressions made in the
floor, as is still done in many farmhouses. But more modern
Japanese homes now use a variety of room-heaters, run by elec-
tricity, gas or paraffin oil (kerosene). The paraffin heaters have
small battery-operated lighters for convenience. In old-style
homes the minute quantity of heat from the *hibachi* was conserved by covering the hole in the floor with a quilt and snuggling
at least arms and legs under it while one sat on the matting
round the edge. The quilt is still used, but safer radiant electric
lamps are often substituted for the *hibachi*. In summer many
Japanese rooms, particularly in inns, are cooled by air con-
ditioners.

When night falls, the women bring out padded quilts from a
cupboard, and spread them on the mat floor, one, two or even
three thicknesses laid underneath as mattresses for softness, and
one or more on top for warmth. When small pillows stuffed with
rice husks are added, the room is turned into a bedroom. In the
morning the quilts are folded up and put away, small trays supported to a height of about 10in are brought in and laid before
each person, and the room is now a dining-room. After breakfast the room may become the husband's study, where he writes
or does accounts on a low table, still kneeling, as he did at breakfast.

It is apparent that such multi-purpose rooms effect a great
saving of space and financial outlay in such a crowded country
as Japan. In fact, one reason why the Japanese middle class can
live comparatively well, can afford cars and labour-saving devices and can still save money is simply that their houses and
furniture cost them so little. Some Japanese inn rooms neatly
combine traditional style in the main room, furnished with mats
and *tokonoma*, with Western style in a wooden verandah. In one
particular instance the verandah had a basin and cupboard at
one end, table and chairs in the middle, and a lavatory and

shower behind a door at the other end. The room and verandah were separated by paper screens and beyond the verandah was the exterior glass window. The governing factor in this lay-out seems to have been the ease of combining the hard wood floor with the plumbing arrangements. The only disadvantage was a certain lack of privacy when shaving.

Foreigners find living on the floor and constantly kneeling a cramping and tiring business. And nowadays it seems a number of Japanese agree with them. Many homes have one or more foreign-style rooms, with tables, chairs and similar furniture, according thus with the Western way of life which is universal in Japanese business offices in the city. On the other hand to most Japanese men returning from work the traditional style spells relaxation. Accustomed to kneeling and squatting from childhood, they prefer life at floor level, where you can go so easily from kneeling to reclining or lying down. I suspect this preference has something to do with the comfort and ease of Japanese dress, ideally suited to life in the mat-covered rooms.

### CLOTHING

The Japanese kimono (the word simply means 'garment' or 'wearing thing') is a wrap-around affair, secured with a sash and essentially similar for men and women. It is inherited from the type of clothing worn in China in the Han Dynasty about the time of Christ, before the Chinese began wearing trousers. The kimono is the ideal leisure wear. It has no buttons or zippers and is never cramping. But worn well by a senior man in dark colours of silk it can be extremely dignified. The bright, dazzling colours of kimono and elaborate feminine sash, or *obi*, worn by a girl can be ravishing. The older women wear becoming greys or subdued lavender tones. There is an infinite variety of shades and pattern designs, but basically only one style.

In contemporary Japan all men working in the cities wear business suits during the day. The majority of women urban workers wear Western dress, but fortunately beautiful kimonos are still to be seen on the streets on festivals and holidays, especially in Kyoto, the city of tradition. Pupils in schools wear uniforms, as do some university students, though to a lesser degree than heretofore. Hippie style is affected by large numbers. Long dark hair, well groomed and styled, gives some students a very attractive, intellectual and sophisticated appearance. In short, all the styles the modern world knows, as well as the traditional style, are to be found in present-day Japan.

## FOOD

Japan relies heavily on the sea for her supply of food. Even today the protein content of the average Japanese diet is derived in greater proportion from sea-food than from meat. Historically this has always been so, for the Japanese are a race of fishermen. Even in prehistoric times early sites of habitation have been identified by the nearby mounds of discarded seashells. Not only do the Japanese enjoy numerous kinds of fish, but they also consume quantities of shell-fish, octopus, squid, eels, lobster, shrimp, seaweed and some whale-meat. Certain fish are eaten raw, cut in thin slices and dipped in various sauces. The farinaceous staple is rice, in the production of which Japan has at last become self-sufficient. Calculations made during World War II indicate that an extremely inexpensive diet containing all the necessary proteins, carbohydrates and vitamins can be derived from the products of the sea plus rice.

Japanese meals are usually served attractively, with separate porcelain or lacquer dishes of various shapes for the different items. These include pickled radish, pickled plums, fish served broiled or cold, as well as raw, seaweed, shell-fish, shrimp, chicken, beef (but not lamb), egg-plant, spinach, cabbage and many kinds of vegetables. There are also clear soups of exotic tastes not known in the West. Soy sauce is used for flavouring. Rice accompanies every meal, as does tea. Japanese tea is a different drink from the darker and stronger Indian variety. It is always taken plain, never with milk or sugar, and forms, in an indefinable way, the ideal companion to rice and the Oriental flavour of Japanese food.


SHOPPING

The most noticeable shops in modern Japan are the vast and crowded department stores which sell everything you can imagine, all the new articles known in other countries as well as new forms of things traditionally Japanese. These department stores have added features little known to us, such as a nursery for children, a zoo, and ski lessons on artificial snow.

At the opposite end of the scale for size are the small shops for connoisseurs in the little lanes of Kyoto, some catering to an exclusive Japanese clientèle, some to foreigners, such as those in Shinmonzen and Furumonzen streets. Here one can buy Japanese prints, silks, porcelain, scroll-paintings and the small carved ivory *netsuke* figures, though genuine examples of the last are becoming scarce. In the upper storeys of great Tokyo office buildings are the hushed and dignified retreats of pearl merchants, who will pour from a casket on to black velvet for you hundreds of pearls all matched for size, and will offer the most varied settings in silver and gold.

In between the bustling giant stores and the small, recherché ones comes all the variety of ordinary shops offering a profusion of goods to a now affluent nation. There are piece-goods of every hue for sale, appliances, heaters, cameras, TV sets, paperbooks and magazines, children's clothes, women's fashions, grocery shops, rubber boots, jewellery both cheap and costly, souvenirs . . . on and on goes the list.

Many shops are located in clusters under a covered arcade, with pedestrian 'malls' closed to vehicular traffic. Scattered among the shops are to be found cafés serving tea, coffee, soft drinks and rather synthetic cakes. Numerous also in the large cities are the *pachinko* parlours, where all types and all ages, fascinated by the chance of minor gambling, go to play the pinball machines.

The Japanese are coming to realise how cold their houses are, and are buying room-heaters of every type, paraffin (kerosene), gas and electric. The portable gas-heaters, with long rubber tubes snaking over the straw-mat floor from an outlet in the wall, would appear to be a fire-hazard; but they are sold in quantity. Refrigerators and air-conditioners are becoming increasingly common. TV sets and radios are taken for granted.

The small neighbourhood shops in the back streets and lanes still form the basis for the Japanese housewife's pattern of buying. This has meant a multiplication of middlemen, each of whom takes his profit in a rather cumbrous and costly system of distribution.

### THE BATH

Taking a bath in Japan is not merely a way to get clean; it is almost a way of life. It is the division between the day of work and the evening of leisure. It is a way to relax and re-create the spirit. It serves the purpose of the cocktail hour, but with fewer harmful effects. There are public baths for those who do not have one in their homes; but those without a bath at home must now be in the minority.

When you take a bath, you fill a small wooden tub, and wash yourself as you stand on the tile floor or sit on a small stool. Only after you have rinsed all the soap off do you get into the tub or plunge-bath and soak. This is an economical way for everyone in the family to enjoy clean, hot water. The accent here is on hot, for the Japanese seem able to bear high temperatures. You sink gingerly down and lie absolutely still, hoping for the best. You emerge red as a lobster, but marvellously refreshed.

Innumerable stories circulate concerning Western shock at mixed bathing in the nude in traditional Japan. The Japanese take a very matter-of-fact attitude to nudity and successfully draw mental lines of privacy round themselves in the crowded life of Japan. But they were shocked in the past by the nude in art, and considered kissing in public quite depraved. Modern films and Western art, of course, have altered present-day attitudes, if not always for the better.

## GARDENS

The art of landscape gardening was one of many cultural imports introduced from China. But the Japanese, in this as in many other spheres, have carried both theory and practice further and developed the art in their own distinctive way. A Japanese garden is the antithesis of the formal and brilliantly coloured garden of European Renaissance style, such as those of Hampton Court or the Palais de Luxembourg. The idea is rather to imitate Nature than to regiment her.

Yet the hand of man is subtly present. The setting, the spacing and the vistas are arranged as carefully as they were by Capability Brown in eighteenth-century England. But the manipulation of nature is much less overt; the art is to conceal art. The best gardens in Japan look almost natural. It is only when one examines them closely that they reveal an improvement on nature—an improvement only in the sense that they bring features normally scattered over the landscape, a tree, a hedge, a waterfall, a curious rock, into narrower compass and harmonious relationship.

A Japanese garden has a few points of rest for the eye, which serve to focus interest. The garden appears to be one whole because these well-known features are related to one another. A path leads to a rock water-basin. A stone lantern stands beneath two trees of contrasting shape. Even the type of fence, of bamboo or of split wood, is chosen for its harmony with the scene. Harmonious asymmetry is preferred to rigid symmetry. Water is almost always present, in the form of a pond or waterfall, or only the contents of a stone basin. Water lends itself to all manner of delightful treatment, with a bridge, stepping-stones, or the murmur of a streamlet falling from a bamboo pipe into a pool.

The gardens of the great are spacious, sumptuous and immaculate. A working couple may have only a very small garden enclosed by a wooden fence; but it seems quite large when seen from inside the house because the proportions of lantern, basin, moss-covered rocks and small pines or maples are exactly right, exactly suited to one another, and create the illusion of distance in a ten-foot space. The garden will seem much larger than it is in fact because of the careful attention paid to scale and arrangement.

Pleasure in gardens links the past with the present, for the Japanese have always valued the presence of living nature in the accessible form that a garden provides. It is well known that the

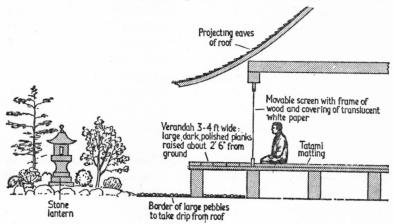

Japanese cultivate miniature gardens, *bonsai*, which flourish indoors, with tiny living trees obtained by root-pruning and other means. What is perhaps not so well known are those features of a Japanese house which bring the real garden indoors, as it were, and make the house in turn a part of the garden. When the screens forming the outside wall of a house are drawn back, there is nothing between the occupant of the house within and the garden outside. His slightly raised position gives him an excellent view of the garden even when seated; and the low verandah without balustrade invites commerce between garden and house.

Many Japanese gardens contain splashes of bright colour at certain seasons of the year—cherry and plum blossoms, wistaria, from lightest to darkest purple, the blue of iris, chrysanthemums

62      *The Japanese: How They Live and Work*

of all colours, and the blood-red of maple leaves in autumn. But for much of the year people are content with, if indeed they do not prefer, the quiet hues of grass, bushes, stones, trees and water. In the great age of Japanese art, the Muromachi period of the fourteenth and fifteenth centuries, a canon of taste was set up which stressed simplicity, restraint, understatement to the point of 'astringency' (a term the Japanese use); and this has influenced Japanese art, including gardens, down to the present day. Thus the garden in front of the original tea-ceremony house consists of nothing but pine-trees and undulating beds of moss, dark green, brown and russet-colour. Nothing quieter, more restful and less flamboyant in the way of a prospect could be devised. Such a garden is ideally suited to the Zen contemplation in which the tea-ceremony took its rise.

Few present-day practitioners of the art of the tea-ceremony can have the advantage of such a setting; but it is still very much a living art. Large manufacturing firms provide, among their extensive recreational facilities, classes in the tea-ceremony for girl operatives in their employ.

The main garden of the Silver Pavilion Temple in Kyoto, in which the original tea-ceremony house stands, is a classic example of a garden of the great age. The Silver Pavilion (it has no silver) stands, a graceful two-storey summer-house and Buddhist temple, at the edge of an ornamental lake. The stepping-stones and flat bridges were gifts to the Shogun Yoshimasa from lords all over Japan. There are winding paths among the maple trees and an expanse of white sand, whose outlines correspond to those of a lake in China famed in literature for its beauty. Some of the sand is raised in a conical mound known as a Moon-Viewing Platform. The whole garden blends in with its natural background in the wooded slopes of a hill.

Let me mention one other famous garden by way of complete contrast. The garden of the Ryoanji Temple in Kyoto is completely stark and abstract. It contains nothing but rocks and sand. The rocks are placed apparently at random but actually with deliberate purpose in pleasing, asymmetrical harmony, in clusters, some vertical, others horizontal. The level white sand in which they are set is raked in parallel lines, with a small series of curves outlining the islands of rock. The whole is precisely limited by a wall with a tiled roof top.

What is the meaning and purpose of this strange garden? Well, to explain anything in Zen, and this is a Zen temple, is regarded as a form of absurdity, and no one can tell exactly what this garden is meant to mean or to do. It is conducive to contemplation. It may call forth ideas. In place of sand, you may imagine water. But ideally the process of Zen contemplation is not an adding but a reducing one. You abstract, take away from the variety of the world and yourself all extraneous, accidental, individual things and return to the undifferentiated reality. The garden of Ryoanji can aid in this process, for it has already got rid of grass, bushes, trees and water, and returned to the basics of sand and rock. But it is not the dull emptiness of the desert and sand alone. It has the rock features on which to fix the mind—and these features are not in mathematical but in artistic relationship. They puzzle and stimulate the mind, and that is a prerequisite of the Zen breakthrough of enlightenment.

Note: If you are in New York, you can see an exact replica of the Ryoanji garden in the Brooklyn Botanic Gardens, as well as another, more typical Japanese garden with lake, trees and bushes.

### THE FAMILY

The ancient form of the extended family was almost universal in East Asia in former days, with grandparents, parents, children and sometimes brothers' families living together in different parts of one large home. This has now given way in Japan to the small family unit of parents, children and perhaps grandmother in one house. Along with this change goes a generation gap, which is now quite pronounced. There is probably less real rebellion on the part of youth in Japan than in the West, but it seems more marked because of the extreme deference to parental and state authority which was evident in the past and is now disappearing. One index of this is that older persons in Japan still feel great reverence for the Emperor, even though he formally renounced his divinity after World War II, whereas young people are comparatively indifferent to him.

Modern Japanese pass their time in work and recreation in ways that are very similar to the Western pattern. Some years ago it would have been customary here to describe a typical day in the life of a Japanese. But nowadays there is little point in such a description. Their cycle of work and leisure in a modern industrialised society is not very different from our own. Most Japanese eat three meals a day, with the principal meal in the evening. The breakfast menu is very similar to that of the other meals. (For food see pp 111 to 113 under Restaurants.) Evening and week-end leisure is spent, as with ourselves, in entertainment, television, cinema, sport, expeditions to the country, skiing, swimming and so on, or just being at home. It might be reasonable to conjecture that children spend more time on lessons and homework than their counterparts in the West, since the competition to enter university is so severe.

The chief difference between the old times and the new in family life is the closer approach to equality now being accorded to women, though their status has not yet reached that of women in the West. A modern proverb circulating in Asia and obviously reflecting a male point of view is that the ideal life is to have an American house on the French Riviera with Chinese food and a Japanese wife. Japanese women still enjoy, if that is the word, a reputation for looking after their men very well; but this does not prevent them today having a sense that they have earned a much greater measure of independence. Between about 1900, when education for girls became more common, and 1940, the height of a Japanese girl increased by the very large amount, for a national average, of 2in. Physical education, better nourishment and less confinement to the house were responsible for the change. Even the last ten years have seen great changes of attitude, as for example in the freedom with which women will speak to strange men, even foreigners, on trains and buses. The advertisements of Japan Air Lines stress the kimono-clad hostesses. But on most flights only one girl at a time wears a kimono, the rest being in Western dress; and she walks with a freer air and no longer with the simpering gait which used to be associated with Japanese women.

Japanese wives certainly enjoy a greater approximation to equality and more companionship with their husbands than in the old days. They leave the seclusion of the home and go out with their husbands. They discuss matters of family and of common concern more nearly on a basis of equality than before. Their husbands even treat them as friends.

Although family life now exhibits what most would consider a new and healthy freedom, there are still many close social bonds in Japanese society which stem from the past. Villages and neighbourhood associations in towns involve and bind individuals in community relationships which are very strong. The obligations or *giri* which Japanese feel to family, clan and village, to teacher, boss or the firm which employs them, have implications and ramifications hard for the Western mind to grasp. Sometimes these bonds are cramping, even stifling; at other times they provide the security of a comfortable framework of mutual support without which individuals would be totally lost.

### FESTIVALS

Certain annual festivals are celebrated today all over Japan and include features which are derived from the ancient past.

The New Year Festival is called *Oshōgatsu*. It is celebrated with varying local elements, but everywhere the girls and women dress in beautiful kimonos, and families take time off from work to observe a holiday, visit shrines and temples and have feasts with special dishes, including cakes of sweet, glutinous rice. In Kyoto at New Year crowds climb up the hill to the Yasaka Shrine at midnight to get fire to re-kindle the family hearth. The shrine and the path leading to it are hung with thousands of lanterns, and the white-robed priests dispense fire from a

flaming pot by kindling the end of a piece of rope for each wor-
shipper. The smouldering rope is kept alight by being whirled
around as the family wends its way slowly home. Before or
after securing the new fire the family may worship at the shrine
by pulling the great white bell-rope to announce their presence
to the god, and then clasping hands and bowing heads in a
short, silent prayer. From the shrine the crowds go farther along
the mountain to a Buddhist temple to see and hear the great
bell in its tower sounded with a deep, gong-like boom by means
of a huge log swung against it on ropes. The sound of the bell
is supposed to give the worshippers a fresh start for the new year
by driving out the 108 evil passions.

The festival of *Setsubun* comes at the end of winter and the beginning of spring. It is concerned with driving out evil spirits
and bringing the new and the good in springtime. Beans are
thrown around in the rooms of the house while this formula is
recited: *Oni wa soto, fuku wa uchi* ('Demons outside, good luck in
the house'). Effigies of insects, worms and other agricultural
pests are burned in bonfires and incantations chanted to drive
away evil from the farms.

Next in the sacred year come two delightful festivals, one for
the girls of the family on the third day of the third month,
3 March, and the other for the boys on the fifth of the fifth,
namely 5 May. At the girls' festival, *Hina-matsuri*, beautifully
dressed small dolls are displayed on tiers of shelves in the home,
in the form of an imperial court, with the emperor and empress
at the top, and their lords, ladies, courtiers, musicians and servants on successive shelves below. The boys have the carp, *koi*,
for a symbol, constructed in paper, suspended outdoors from a
high pole, having a large open mouth and a hollow body
through which the wind can blow. These gaily coloured carp
moving in the wind look for all the world like real fish swimming.
The carp is admired as a strong fish that swims with vigour
upstream, and thus forms both a model for a boy in overcoming
difficulties and a wish of his parents for him.

Perhaps the greatest festival of the year is *Obon*, commemorat-
ing the temporary return to earth and home of the ancestral

spirits once each year at the end of July. The ancestors are welcomed back, and entertained with offerings of food and sometimes with dances in their honour. In some villages a path is cut through the grass to lead the spirits down from the mountain, where they are presumed to dwell, and bonfires are lighted to guide them on their way. Offerings are made not only to the friendly, family spirits but also to hungry ghosts who have no one to care for them. This is done so that they may not be angry and harm the village. At the conclusion of the festival the spirits are sent on their way back to their abode with suitable gifts and ceremonies.

The older structure of the ritual provides for the gods or spirits to answer, during their short stay in the human world, questions concerning the future, as to possible sickness, flood or disaster, and the means of preventing them. The answers are conveyed through an inspired medium. But this element has largely been forgotten in the present-day celebrations of *obon*.

Lastly, there is another festival connected with children on 15 November, known as *Shichigosan*. The word means 'seven, five, three'. Girls dressed in bright kimonos are presented at the shrine of the Shinto deity on the fifteenth day of the month at the ages of three and seven, and boys at the age of five. This festival is observed more particularly in the Kanto area round Tokyo.

# 4

# *How They Work*

THE simplest answer to the question of how the Japanese work is to say they work hard. Few peoples in the world are more industrious. As late as the eighteenth century a Japanese farmer's wife would be reprimanded for taking time off to go for a walk in the afternoon. Noble landowners did not expect to grant to their peasants more than barely enough to keep them alive; the rest of the grain production went for rent, taxes and dues. Holidays still are few and the week-end is a recent innovation. Nowadays, however, the regular hours worked each week in industry are in the moderate range of 41 to 46.

### FARMING

Farmers and peasants have traditionally had to work hard, since only 17 per cent of Japan's area is arable land; the rest is mountain and forest. As the population increased in the modern era Japan had to import rice from South-East Asia; but now she has again become self-sufficient due to the introduction of high-yield and disease-resistant crops, the use of chemical fertilisers and pesticides and the widespread mechanisation of agriculture. The number of small farm and garden tractors and powered cultivators grew from ½ million in 1959 to 3 million in 1968. But even with modern aids the cultivation of rice, the chief grain-crop, remains very dependent on human labour. The rice-paddies of irregular shape nestle into the folds of the hills, each one carefully levelled, interspersed with water-channels, and surrounded with low barriers of earth to retain the water. The new shoots must be planted out into standing water. On higher slopes in the warm south are carefully tended tea-bushes, and down in the valleys the glossy green leaves and bright yellow fruit of orange groves, where the fruit remains on the trees all winter and is picked in the spring. This landscape, so lovingly shaped, tidied and tended by man for countless generations, would have delighted the civilised eyes of the Augustans of Rome or of Dr Johnson's England. Yet just for this reason, the necessity of restraint and toil, the romantics of Japan, monks, artists, recluses and poets, escaped to do their work and take their delight in the mountain fastnesses and forest recesses.

Rice is by far the most important farm crop of Japan (14 million metric tons in 1968). But other crops in order of importance are potatoes (4 million metric tons), cabbage (3·8 million metric tons), sweet potatoes (3 million metric tons), mandarin oranges (2·3 million metric tons), water-melons, apples and wheat. Hokkaido, the northernmost island, provides pasture for an important dairy industry, and the Japanese now consume milk and cheese as never in the past.

Timber of good quality was always in abundant supply in Japan's past from the great forests. These forests owed their preservation in part to the fact that much of the ground upon which they grew was too steep or otherwise unsuitable for agriculture. Nowadays the demands of modern industry have entirely changed the picture. Japan in 1969 had to import 35·8 million metric tons of wood and lumber and only exported 0·1 million tons of timber in the form of plywood.

Out of a work-force of 50 million persons in Japan, 9·5 million, or just under 20 per cent, are employed in agriculture, forestry and fishing. The proportion so employed in the UK is only 1·8 per cent and in the USA 6·2 per cent.

FISHING

Fishing is a major industry in Japan, and has been throughout her history. In 1969 Japanese fishermen landed 2 million

E

metric tons of cod and haddock, 1·2 million metric tons of the mackerel family, and 1·3 million metric tons of shell-fish. The most varied types of aquatic creatures are caught and eaten—whales, fish large and small, octopus, squid, eels, lobster, crab, shrimp and shell-fish of all kinds. They are caught by the most varied means—harpoon, net, hook and line, bait, trap, trained cormorants and women who dive for the awabi shell-fish.

The ancient method of fishing with cormorants has been retained here and there, mainly as a tourist attraction. Flares in the prows of the boats attract the fish, and trained cormorants, slender birds which are extremely agile under water, catch them in their beaks. The birds are attached to the boat by long lines and have a ring round their necks to prevent them swallowing the fish. As to the women divers, their craft is extremely old, and their semi-clad beauty and the mystery of their life has been the subject of many Japanese prints and stories. The young woman descends with the aid of stone weights and a line attached to a boat above, often manned by her husband. She wears goggles and carries an angular piece of wood to pry the large shell-fish off the rocks. Those operating in shallower water do not use a boat, but have a wooden tub floating on the surface to receive their catch. They are compelled by law to continue with the old method of diving and not to use aqualung equipment so as to maintain the catch within limits and not deplete the shell-fish population. Women undertake this work rather than men, because their layer of subcutaneous fat retains body heat longer in the cold water. Nowadays, understandably, most wear skin-diving suits for extra protection against cold.

## INDUSTRY

Manufacturing, beginning much later in Japan than in the West, now occupies 13·5 million persons or 27 per cent of the work force. In the UK the percentage is 38·9 and in the USA about the same as that of Japan, namely 26·9 per cent. (It should be noted, however, that these and the following figures

in the tables 1 and 2 are not fully comparable owing to varia-
tions in methods of statistical compilation, for which I have
endeavoured to compensate.)

Table 1   Comparative manpower statistics
(millions employed, year 1969)

|  | Japan | UK | USA |
|---|---|---|---|
| Agriculture, forestry, fishing | 9·5 | 0·4 | 4·6 |
| Mining | 0·2 | 0·5 | 0·6 |
| Manufacture | 13·5 | 9·1 | 20·1 |
| Construction and public works | 3·7 | 1·6 | 3·4 |
| Commerce | 11·3 | 3·2 | 18·2 |
| Transportation and public utilities | 3·4 | 2·0 | 4·5 |
| Services, including government | 8·8 | 6·3 | 23·3 |
| Totals (corrected) | 50·4 | 23·6 | 74·7 |

Table 2   Comparative manpower statistics
(percentage of total work-force)

| Japan | | UK | | USA | |
|---|---|---|---|---|---|
| Manufacture | 27·0 | Manufacture | 38·9 | Services, incl government | 31·1 |
| Commerce | 22·6 | Services, incl government | 27·3 | Manufacture | 26·9 |
| Agriculture, forestry, fishing | 19·0 | Commerce | 13·9 | Commerce | 24·4 |
| Services, incl government | 17·6 | Transportation and utilities | 8·7 | Agriculture, forestry, fishing | 6·2 |
| Construction | 7·4 | Construction | 6·9 | Transportation and utilities | 6·0 |
| Transportation and utilities | 6·8 | Mining | 2·2 | Construction | 4·5 |
| Mining | 0·4 | Agriculture, forestry, fishing | 1·8 | Mining | 1·0 |

From these tables the signs are clear that Japan, for good or
ill, has fully come of age as a modern industrial nation, since
manufacture, as in the UK, is the largest sector of employment.

It is noticeable, however, that the number employed in primary production in agriculture, forestry and fishing is still high, in third place, as contrasted with the UK, where this sector comes in last place. Japan grows all the rice she requires and 85 per cent of her total food needs, in marked contrast to Great Britain.

### ECONOMIC GROWTH

Since Japan has to survive as an island nation with poor mineral resources, she must invest skilled labour in her products

*Table 3    Industrial production index*

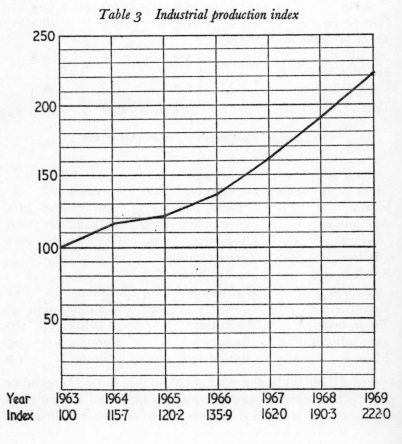

| Year | 1963 | 1964 | 1965 | 1966 | 1967 | 1968 | 1969 |
|------|------|------|------|------|------|------|------|
| Index | 100 | 115·7 | 120·2 | 135·9 | 162·0 | 190·3 | 222·0 |

to enhance their value. The more skilled the labour required, as in the precision work in cameras and optical goods, electronics and automobiles, the better the return on a given amount of raw material, much of which has to be imported. As is well known, Japan's rate of economic growth has been phenomenal. Taking 1963 as 100 the industrial production index has gone as shown in Table 3 opposite:

The recent Prime Minister, Eisaku Sato, and his Liberal Democratic Party (politically conservative) electioneered on the promise of an annual 10 per cent rate of economic growth. This has been more than fulfilled, as this graph indicates:

*Table 4    Gross national product (in thousand million yen)*

| Year | 1959 | 1960 | 1961 | 1962 | 1963 | 1964 | 1965 | 1966 | 1967 | 1968 | 1969 |
|------|------|------|------|------|------|------|------|------|------|------|------|
| GNP | 18·0 | 20·3 | 23·3 | 24·6 | 27·8 | 30·6 | 32·3 | 36·0 | 40·7 | 46·3 | 52·1 |

(Source: *Statistical Yearbook for Asia and the Far East: 1970*, United Nations)

Japan has therefore more than tripled the amount of her gross national product in ten years. She now ranks third in the world in this respect after the USA and the USSR.

Without entering into the more arcane regions of economic theory, it seems evident that at least four factors help to account for this unprecedented economic advance: first, the hard work and determination alluded to at the beginning of this chapter; second, substantial economic aid from America after the war, and an enlightened occupation policy; third, harmonious labour relations and hence an almost total absence of work stoppages; and fourth, a pattern of heavy financial borrowing for rapid expansion and the mutual confidence to make this work. The last two factors deserve some further brief examination.

## LABOUR UNIONS

There are labour unions in Japan, but over 90 per cent of them are what union men from the West would consider a contradiction in terms, namely company unions. The company provides facilities for union activity, in some cases arranges withholding from pay for union dues, and even has the company president acting, with the agreement of the workers, as the union president. It will be seen that under these conditions strikes and job action are not of frequent occurrence and unions usually confine themselves to calling attention to workers' grievances.

On the other hand, workers enjoy almost complete job security and can count on pay rising steadily with seniority. Once a man is taken on by a certain firm he can practically count on the job for life. He is similarly expected by the firm to stick to the job. The larger firms provide free recreational facilities and sometimes free housing for their workers. Western critics would call the whole arrangement paternalism; but it fits the Japanese scene and stems from her feudal past. The feudal system itself was founded upon personal and family loyalty, and thus the whole of Japanese life is interwoven with bonds of mutual obligation which carry over, even in attenuated forms, into the relationships of modern economic life. Thus in small firms, for example, which cannot afford elaborate facilities for recreation, the manager-worker bond may prove beneficial and supportive, as when the head of the firm and his wife take a dozen girl workers with them to the sea-shore for two weeks' holiday at the firm's expense. It would be a mistake, however, to assume that strain and conflict are entirely absent from the economic system of Japan or from its labour-management relationships. Large firms perforce lose the personal touch; there is a pronounced generation gap; many firms in large urban centres are developing more independent unions; and there is a febrile 'rat-race' and 'get-ahead' atmosphere which encourages conflict.

## CAPITAL

As to the fourth factor, the practice of borrowing capital, a situation prevails which would strike horror to the hearts of conservative board chairmen in the West. In October 1971 William V. Rapp stated:

*For the typical Japanese firm, less than 20 per cent of total capital employed is owned capital (equity and retained earnings) with more than 80 per cent of total capital employed being made up of short and long term borrowings and the financing of trade receivables. United States companies characteristically obtain most of their capital from equity and retained earnings, while debt comprises a third or less of total output.*

('How the Japanese Run a Business', *New York Times*, 17 October 1971)

## BUSINESS STRUCTURE

The structure of Japanese business has one interesting feature which distinguishes it from its Western counterparts, namely the greater use of sub-contracting to small specialist firms, whose entire production is absorbed by the large firm. The large firm then looks after part of the manufacture and the assembly, marketing and development of the finished product.

This appears to be an outgrowth of a pre-modern Japanese practice of village and home industry which expanded greatly under the pressure of World War II military requirements. The system involves a risk to the small firms whose solvency is entirely dependent on the goodwill and success of the larger firm. But the small firms find the risk an acceptable one, since they need to support neither a sales organisation nor facilities for research and development. These are both provided by the parent firm.

The history of industrial enterprise in Japan since modernisation in the latter half of the nineteenth century is a fascinating one, although it falls outside the scope of this book. (Those interested are referred to works by W. G. Beasley, Hugh Borton and William W. Lockwood.) Large industrial firms, known as *zaibatsu* ('financial cliques') developed early, were closely associated with the government and played a considerable part in the formation of national policy. They were forced to split up into independent firms by order of the occupying powers after World War II, but new combinations and conglomerates have now been formed, closely similar to the old.

## UNEMPLOYMENT

Unemployment has never been a serious problem in Japan. At the present time less than 2 per cent of the Japanese labour force is without work. From 1962 to 1968 inclusive nearly ¾ million new jobs were created annually. This is six times greater than the job creation level in France, Germany or England (Guillan: *The Japanese Challenge*, p 102). Japan is still going through her industrial revolution and it has overlapped with the new technological revolution. In 1968 the number of jobs available in Japan each month exceeded the number of monthly job applications by 130,000 (*Japan Economic Yearbook*, 1969, p 249). Thus there is now a serious labour shortage.

### FOREIGN TRADE—EXPORTS

Begin with a simple but staggering pair of figures: in 1955 Japanese exports were worth $2,004 million; in 1970 they were worth $19,319 million. These goods were distributed to all areas of the world in the following proportions in descending order:

*Table 5    Exports by area, 1969*

|  | per cent |
|---|---|
| To North America | 34·0 |
| To South-East Asia | 27·8 |
| To Western Europe | 12·8 |
| To Africa | 7·2 |
| To Latin America | 5·9 |
| To the Communist Bloc | 4·8 |
| To Oceania, including Australia and New Zealand | 3·9 |
| To West Asia | 3·5 |

(Source: Japan Foreign Trade Organization, *The Foreign Trade of Japan, 1970*, p 9)

Exports to the USA in 1969 reached almost $5,000 million, up 21·3 per cent over the previous year. The value of the goods which the United States receives from Japan is seven times the amount which Japan exports to any other single country (*Japan Economic Yearbook, 1969*, p 261). The proportion of Japan's exports sent to the USA out of her total exports decreased, however, in 1970, representing 31 per cent instead of 34 per cent, while her exports to South-East Asia increased from 27·8 to 30 per cent. From the Japanese point of view this is a healthy trend, making her less dependent upon the United States. The kind of goods exported to developed countries such as the USA and Western Europe are the products of advanced engineering in the form of cars, radios, steel and ships, whereas those to developing countries comprise textiles, industrial machinery, fertilisers and other chemicals.

As a contrast to the present-day sophisticated electronic items and major products of heavy industry produced by Japan, it is instructive to compare a list of much simpler, light industrial products contained in an International Labour Office publication of 1934 including such items as matches, pottery, electric bulbs, watches and clocks, fountain pens and lacquer. To many people this 1934 list, with toys and perhaps radios added, is still the image of Japanese industry; but in fact the picture has changed out of all recognition. One basic reason Japan has been able to trade so successfully since World War II in such varied fields is that she has instituted a strict system of quality control, enabling her to compete in reliability of items as well as in their price.

Japan, however, is still very sensitive to charges of 'dumping' and unfair competition, as witness such sentences as these in the introduction to *Foreign Trade of Japan, 1970* published by the Japan External Trade Organization: 'It is a great pity that some people abroad have misunderstandings concerning the Japanese economy and foreign trade policies . . . We, the editors, are very pleased if this publication will prove of any help to those willing to understand real Japan . . .'

What is most notable to the economist in the trend of modern Japanese industry is the shift, because of world demand, from labour-intensive to capital-intensive industries. 'The higher the value-added per employee, the more capital-intensive the industry, and the lower the value-added per employee, the more labour-intensive the industry is.' (From H. B. Lary: *Imports of Manufactures from Less-Developed Countries*, New York 1968, p 14.) Thus examples of labour-intensive products would be textiles and toys, and of capital-intensive products railway vehicles, steel and ships. It is precisely in these latter products of heavy industry that the most significant recent expansion in Japan has taken place.

### SHIPBUILDING

Of the world tonnage of ships launched in 1971 almost half (48 per cent) came from Japanese yards. Next in sequence but far behind in percentage came, in this order, Sweden, West Germany and Great Britain. The mammoth tankers, of well over 300,000 tons, are built in Nagasaki, which began as a small port developed by the Jesuits in the sixteenth century. These tankers are so large that they have to be built in two sections. The bow and the stern are launched separately and joined together when in the water. Prefabricated elements weighing 600 tons apiece are lifted by two great cranes into a drydock and there assembled. Before one ship is finished, the elements of another are being welded into sections by simple automatic welders invented by Japanese. They work on a gravity principle and five can be tended by one man.

### FOREIGN TRADE—IMPORTS

Japanese imports have increased from $2,470 million in 1955 to $18,883 million in 1970. Dividing these imports into groups of commodities expressed as percentages of total imports yields the following:

*Table 6   Commodities as percentage of total imports, 1970*

| | | |
|---|---|---|
| Raw materials | 35·9 | with lumber and iron ore among the largest items |
| Manufactured goods | 29·1 | |
| Mineral fuels | 20·3 | with crude oil much the largest item |
| Foodstuffs | 14·3 | |
| Re-imports | 0·4 | |

(Source: *Foreign Trade of Japan, 1970*, p 12)

For the iron ore vital to the steel industry Oceania, including Australia, became for the first time in 1969 Japan's largest supplier, contributing 28 per cent of the total of 83·2 million tons of iron ore imported. Imported non-ferrous metal ores amounted to almost 12 million tons, and here, for the first time, South-East Asia outstripped North America as the chief supplier. This and other related facts concerning increase of Japanese exports to South-East Asia have evident significance for the future of world politics.

Crude oil valued at $1,907 million was imported to Japan in 1969, 90 per cent of it from West Asia (the Near and Middle East). But a slightly increased proportion of crude oil came from South-East Asia, because this oil contains a little less sulphur, which decreases the pollution hazard. Japan suffers severely from pollution, as the penalty for rapid and heedless industrialisation. But public opinion is forcing the government to take some action against offending firms. In the vicinity of Tokyo some factories, especially paper-pulp factories, have made the air and water so polluted that trees and grass have died and fish have left this part of the coast for cleaner waters, necessitating long trips by fishing boats. Tokyo traffic police have access to oxygen supplies when overwhelmed by traffic fumes.

### BALANCE OF TRADE

It is quite plain from what has been tabulated above that the Japanese economy is in a very strong state financially. The trade balances by geographical areas (Table 7) reflect this overall

*Table 7   Japan's trade balances ( $ millions)*

|  | 1964 | 1970 |
|---|---|---|
| With total world | −1,265 | + 436 |
| Of which, with USA | − 494 | + 394 |
| Western Europe | + 49 | + 955 |
| Republic of Korea, Taiwan, Hong Kong, Thailand, Singapore | + 497 | +2,241 |
| Other South and East Asia | − 8 | − 341 |
| Middle East | − 668 | −1,703 |
| Latin America and Africa | − 309 | − 744 |
| Australia and Canada | − 561 | −1,277 |

(Source: *General Agreement on Tariffs and Trade, Study number 2, Japan's Economic Expansion 1955–70*, Geneva 1971, p 34)

strength and the change from 1964 to 1970 is dramatic. The negatives in the lower part of the table occur opposite countries from which Japan imports raw materials.

## WAGES AND STANDARD OF LIVING

The Japanese on the whole are not a luxury-loving people. They have learned to do without, and indeed have placed a positive value on simplicity. Elements of their life are still simple. For instance, the average Japanese spends less on home and furniture than his opposite number in the West. But modern labour-saving devices have become extremely popular, and cars, electric appliances, radios, television sets and sound equipment show enormous sales figures. The Akihabara district of Tokyo has a large semi-open-air market area; but it sells not vegetables but colour TV sets, heaters and automatic washers in unimaginable numbers. There are more colour TV sets per capita of the population in Japan than in the USA.

The large increase in sales abroad is based upon a more than adequate increase in the home market to provide a healthy economy, for the internal sales (wholesale) in 1966 were nearly 15 times the value of the goods exported. Wages have increased at a much faster pace than consumer prices, which has meant a dramatic rise in the standard of living. A considerable portion of the surplus goes into savings in the average Japanese family.

*Table 8    Wage and price indices, with 1963 as 100*

|                 | 1963 | 1966 | 1970 |
|-----------------|------|------|------|
| Wages           | 100  | 140  | 203  |
| Consumer prices | 100  | 117  | 136  |

(Source: *Japan's Economic Expansion 1955–70*)

It should be noted, however, that since wages increase with seniority, the starting wage for a young working family may be quite low.

SUMMARY

Japan's strategy of industrial development has paid off. Internally the standard of living has risen, labour has been mobilised and trained, and productivity has grown rapidly. Externally there has been a considerable penetration into foreign markets, although this penetration is concentrated into a comparatively narrow band of products. Increase in exports has been achieved without a corresponding rise in dependence upon imports.

The need is now for Japan to broaden the base of her exports by a greater range of exported products, to reduce import restrictions and abandon discriminatory trade policies. There will almost certainly be increased trade with the People's Republic of China in the immediate future. There will probably be more mutual exchange of investment and technology with foreign nations. As the GATT Study predicts: 'The role of Japan as a low labour-cost supplier of finished manufactures will be gradually taken over by other countries.' (*Japan's Economic Expansion 1955–70*, p 50.) Japan's performance in modernisation in the last one hundred years may well serve as a model to present-day developing countries.

# 5

# *How They Learn*

ALMOST all Japanese are literate, in the sense that they can read and write, even though their language is complicated and difficult. Two very different factors have combined to produce this desirable result: (1) that the difficulty of the borrowed Chinese script is reduced by the use of a Japanese syllabary, functioning like an alphabet; and (2) that the government adopted a determined policy of universal compulsory education in modern times. Even so, the very high rate of literacy, over 98 per cent, must be due also to motives which lie deep in the nature of the Japanese, such as their industry and innate curiosity.

## HISTORICAL STAGES OF EDUCATION

The roots of society and culture in Japan extend far into the past and still derive strength from tradition. Historically education in Japan may be said to have passed through four stages, none of which is totally obsolete, and all of which still affect, in greater or less degree, the children in the schools and the youth in the colleges and the streets.

They are, in brief:

A *The Traditional Stage* Inspiration for this stage was derived from China and Confucius, and the emphasis was placed upon literature and the humanities, and upon the ethics of duty, loyalty and filial piety. Historians of Japan have stressed the influence of Shinto and Buddhism, but less than justice has been done to the strong Confucian element, introduced officially as early as the seventh century and at its height in the realm of education in the eighteenth and early nineteenth centuries.

B *The Modernising Stage* Following the Meiji Restoration of 1868, the statesmen of the new Japan deliberately borrowed from the West a number of institutions which they felt could be best adapted to their country's purposes—a constitution from Bismarck in Prussia, a navy from Great Britain, and education moulded largely on the American pattern, which they had seen well exemplified in some excellent mission schools, particularly in pioneer schools for girls. To this they added parts of the administrative apparatus drawn from France and Germany. The incompatibilities in these various borrowings struck the Japanese less than they would outsiders, for all was reduced to order under the aegis of 'the Japanese spirit'.

One of the more picturesque and influential figures of this dynamic age was Yukichi Fukuzawa, founder of the school which became Keio University, the first private university in Japan. He describes his early struggles with 'the strange letters written sideways', and the fury of his samurai father that his children were being taught arithmetic in a small private school. 'It is abominable,' the father exclaimed, 'that innocent children

---

Sumo wrestling has a long history in Japan, and the seasonal professional tournaments are still immensely popular. A wrestler wins when he succeeds in shoving his opponent out of the 15ft ring or causes any part of his opponent's body to touch the platform. The sport is steeped in Shinto religious tradition, and the referee in the centre of the ring at this opening ceremony is clad in priestly dress.

This scene by the famous Takarazuka all-girl troupe is based on the popular Kabuki theatre style of colourful drama. The chorus represent farmer-warriors, some with singlestick weapons, some with sickles. The castle in the background and the cherry blossom both signify the life of the warrior, for the cherry blossom falls in its prime before ever the leaves of maturity appear.

should be taught to use numbers—the tool of merchants. There is no telling what the teacher may do next.' (Eiichi Kiyooka: *The Autobiography of Yukichi Fukuzawa*, Columbia University Press, 1966, p 3.) He took his children out of school. But numbers have come into their own in Japan. Your reserved seat on 'the fastest train in the world' is now assigned to you by a computer.

C *The Military Stage* When the militarists gained control of the governmental process in the 1930s, there was a great change. Military training was compulsory for boys in all schools, and texts in ethics and history stressed fanatic patriotism and the mystique of emperor-worship. The respected Professor Minobe of Tokyo University, whose books were the standard texts in political science, was disgraced for designating the Emperor as 'an organ of government' and not a god manifest. This phase is so well known that it is scarcely necessary to underline it further.

D *The Present Stage* After the defeat of 1945, an entirely new approach to education was adopted and new textbooks were written. The change was initiated by the American occupation authorities, but it was accepted without demur by the Japanese. Democratic rather than authoritarian trends prevailed, and

---

A contrast to Kabuki is the classical Nō theatre. There is no scenery and almost no help from props. But the severe masks (worn by young women, old men and demons but not by male adults) and the gorgeous brocade costumes give a remote and tragic air to the action. The legendary themes, the mimed dances and the presence of a chorus are at times reminiscent of classical Greek tragedy.

A Japanese artist putting pressure on the brush to give a broad stroke on the rice paper. The finest line can also be drawn by a light touch on the traditional tapering brush of badger-hairs set in bamboo. Painting and calligraphy are regarded as two aspects of one art. Both are determined by the severe condition, 'Once drawn, beyond recall'. No touching up is possible with this paper.

F

emphasis was directed away from official dogma and toward the training of children to reach their own conclusions and form their own convictions. All courses in morality and ethics were dropped and courses in social science were substituted. Both China and Japan have been used to a state orthodoxy, and it may seem regrettable that some course with an acceptable moral content could not have been worked out to give Japanese children some of the guidance to which they were accustomed.

It is admittedly a question whether school instruction can accomplish much in the moral field. Some maintain this can only be done by family and church or temple. But all children, and perhaps Japanese children particularly, are grateful for clear guide-lines, even if only to react against. It is at least possible that a clearer moral lead in the schools, though without compulsion, might have helped to eliminate some of the malaise and uncertainty of students in post-war Japan.

It must at the same time be said that the Japanese authorities, in full control since the Peace Treaty of 1951, have not seen fit to make any change in this regard in the policy set up under the occupation authorities. An official government pamphlet states:

> *The Law emphasises the importance of political knowledge and of religious tolerance in the development of sound citizens but it specifically prohibits any link between political parties or religions and education.*

The problem is how to combine moral guidance in the schools with religious freedom—and this is an acute problem for Western countries as well as for Japan.

## THE PRESENT EDUCATIONAL SYSTEM

The educational system in present-day Japan is divided into five levels: kindergarten, 1 to 3 years; elementary school, 6 years; lower secondary, 3 years; upper secondary, 3 years; university, normally 4 years. Education is compulsory for 9 years and free for all children between the ages of 6 and 15 at public elementary and lower secondary schools. Thirty per cent of upper secondary pupils attend private schools. Out of a total population of 103 million, just over 20 million children were attending schools from kindergarten to the upper secondary schools in May 1969, while 1,355,000 students were enrolled in the universities. It is claimed that 99·9 per cent of the children in the compulsory age group are registered as attending school. It is also claimed in government publications that education is decentralised and under the control of local boards of education. But the members of these boards are appointed by the head of the local governing authority; the course of study upon which local curricula must be planned is laid down by the Ministry of Education; and textbooks, although selected locally, must be from among those authorised by the Ministry. Local autonomy is thus somewhat limited. (Statistics above from *The Japan of Today*, 1970 edn, Japanese Government publication, pp 93–4.)

The numbers of schools and students at the different levels, showing differences between 1960 and 1968, are as follows:

| Table 9 Level | Number of schools | | Number of students | |
|---|---|---|---|---|
| | *(all in thousands)* | | | |
| | 1960 | 1968 | 1960 | 1968 |
| Pre-school | 7·1 | 10·0 | 742 | 1,420 |
| Primary | 22·7 | 25·3 | 12,591 | 9,383 |
| Secondary, total | 17·6 | 16·3 | 9,139 | 9,565 |
| general | 13·0 | 11·5 | 7,781 | 7,701 |
| vocational/ technical | 4·6 | 4·8 | 1,359 | 1,864 |
| College/university, including technical colleges | ·5 | ·9 | 712 | 1,395 |
| Totals | 65·5 | 68·8 | 23,184 | 21,763 |
| Student-teacher ratio, overall | | | 28:1 | 21:1 |

The figures above reveal one or two interesting trends, namely:

Pre-school—pupils doubled;

Primary—number of schools up, number of pupils markedly down, presumably due to the tapering off in the birth-rate. From 1949 to 1959 the birth-rate in Japan dropped dramatically, from about 33 per thousand to about 17 per thousand. (The Japanese birth-rate of 17·2 per thousand, 1960, is comparable to the level of births in other major industrial countries: Great Britain 17·5, USA 17·8, Italy 18·4.)

Secondary—number of schools down, and number of students slightly up. But note that all the increase is located in the vocational/technical secondary schools.

College/university—number of colleges and students almost doubled.

### SCHOOL CURRICULUM

Turning to individual subjects in the school curriculum today, it is evident that science and technology are receiving increased attention. English language study is also rising, and the study of other foreign languages is proportionately slightly lower. Young doctors, for instance, no longer have to study German, although this was always the rule in the past. Three to four hours a week for six years are devoted to the study of English in school. Young Japanese are very earnest in their efforts to learn this flexible, illogical, intractable language. One law student I spoke to in Japan recently confessed to having learned all the contents of a small English dictionary by heart.

At least three national newspapers in Japan publish English-language editions and their readership is certainly Japanese as well as foreign. When I addressed an English-speaking society in Nagasaki (they are common all over Japan), I was struck by the variety of background and employment among the thirty or so young men and women attending the meeting. They included a hotel receptionist, a shipyard welder, several economics majors in the university, a librarian and a secretary in the city hall.

I enquired about the teaching of Japanese history in the schools. It was distorted under the military régime; then it was said to have been minimised after the war. It now seems to be what we would call 'normally taught', with due pride but without extreme jingoism, yielding an average knowledge of the subject. History undoubtedly suffers from competition with other subjects in a crowded curriculum. There is no evidence whatever that anything in the present teaching of history is leading to a revival of militarism. Speculation of this topic keeps cropping up in newspapers outside Japan—a kind of expected sensationalism; but it is discounted as a threat in a balanced, well-reasoned United States government report issued since the Yukio Mishima suicide. The main argument of this report is that not only students but the great majority of the Japanese people who have grown up since World War II will not let any government in Japan travel far down the road towards the waging of aggressive war. No one can predict the future turns of power politics in the Pacific, but the likelihood that a frenetic but small right-wing group will revive militarism as the dominant philosophy in Japan is probably minimal.

### THE JAPANESE LANGUAGE

Japanese belongs to the Ural-Altaic group of languages in the northern part of the Eurasian land mass, and has distant relationships to Magyar and Finnish. As a spoken language (polysyllabic and inflected) it has no affinity with spoken Chinese (monosyllabic and uninflected); and here begins a complication. About the sixth century AD the Japanese, who had no writing, began using the written characters (ideograms) of China. For most characters there are thus at least two pronunciations, one a native Japanese word, the other with the same meaning as the Japanese word but with a pronunciation similar to the original Chinese sound. The use of one or other the pronunciation is usually determined by the context or the intellectual level of discourse, the Chinese form being generally the more learned or the more formal. Sometimes only one form or the other is ever used.

Occasionally matters become still more involved, when one written character has to stand for several different meanings. Thus 生 is the character associated with birth and growth, and is pronounced *sheng* in standard Chinese, *shō* in the Sino-Japanese form, and in several ways in native Japanese, each with a different meaning: as *iku*, to live; *umaru*, to bear a child; *nama*, raw (as a vegetable *grows* in the field before it is cooked); and so on up to about ten different pronunciations. The phenomenon of borrowed and transferred meanings, literal, metaphorical and so on, is common in any language; but in European languages the written form and the pronunciation are identical in all cases, and only the meaning varies according to the use and context. In Japanese both pronunciation and meaning of one written form vary.

In practice, of course, Japanese usage can be learned and is not so bad as it sounds. But the language is among the most difficult in the world, both for foreigners and even for the Japanese themselves. One great aid is the use of the *kana* syllabary to help in pronunciation and to indicate verb-endings and other grammatical elements for which there is no other written character form. (This device is not available to the Chinese, for reasons which it would take too long to explain, but which are inherent in the nature of the Chinese language itself.) Native Japanese words are entirely made up of syllables consisting of a consonant followed by a vowel, thus, ma, mi, mu, me, mo; ra, ri, ru, re, ro; and so on. There are only 10 consonants used with the 5 vowels, and a final –n. Some of the combinations are not used, which results in a total of 47 *kana* syllables. These are represented by shorthand contractions of Chinese characters, said to have been invented by a Japanese Buddhist monk in the eighth century AD on the analogy of Sanskrit letters. But these symbols, unlike the true borrowed Chinese characters (or *kanji*), have only sound and no meaning. In other words they take the place of a Japanese alphabet. For good measure the Japanese have two sets of *kana*, the simpler *katakana* similar to our printed script, and *hiragana*, slightly more florid and similar to our cursive script.

## LANGUAGE DIFFERENCES

Thus to a foreigner written Japanese presents, to say the least, considerable difficulties. Spoken Japanese of a simple kind can be acquired fairly easily, with a vocabulary sufficient to get along in shopping and in finding one's way around; and even a little Japanese is very useful in oiling the social wheels. But as soon as one enters upon the realm of ideas, abstract discussion or specialised vocabulary, difficulties begin to mount. The reasons for this are interesting, inherent in the differing psychology of Japanese and Westerners.

We in the West tend to pride ourselves on being direct, clear, definitive and what we call 'honest'. The Japanese stress harmony, respect, consideration for another's feelings. Thus communicating concepts is far more complicated for an English speaker than doing the corresponding thing in French or German. The difficulty is that Japanese thought-processes, and therefore language structures, differ radically from Western ones. To translate a sentence you must take it to bits and reconstruct it in the way the Japanese would approach its real meaning. The Japanese value vagueness, partly from reasons of politeness, and dislike statements that are too clear and definite. They often leave sentences hanging in mid-air, ending with 'but . . .', which acts as a loophole, as though to say, 'There may be another point of view on this, and I shall not insist upon mine.' They avoid even the use of personal pronouns, and have a number of shades of probability and possibility expressed by verb-forms. 'It is not necessary in Japanese to express, or even to have a clear conception of, the subject of a sentence,' as the introduction to a Japanese grammar book puts it.

Their language naturally has a logic of its own, but it is not the Greek logic of precision, exact definition founded on either/or. The Japanese prefer suggesting, hinting, indicating a direction of thought or intention of the will, but leaving ways out for the speaker or hearer in the dialogue to retreat or change direction without losing face. And if the lack of pronouns mentioned above seems puzzling, it is well to remember that the polite form of speech is sufficient to indicate that the other person, you, is being referred to, while the humbler form is used by the speaker of himself. Prefixes, endings and special words are used to indicate degrees of politeness, eg when a child is speaking to an adult, or when old and familiar friends are speaking to one another on a level. 'Man's language' and 'woman's language' are sometimes referred to in popular accounts of Japan. They are not, of course, entirely different; simply that the women use the more deferential and courteous terms and verb-forms, while the men speak more directly and brusquely. The extreme terms of deference are less used than in former days.

When learning Japanese, or even memorising Japanese names, it is a help to realise that almost all components of words are syllables beginning with a consonant and ending with a vowel. Thus the name of a famous historical person is broken up in this way: MI–NA–MO–TO YO–RI–TO–MO. Here the surname Minamoto comes first according to the old Chinese and Japanese practice. But nowadays it is usual to follow the Western custom and put the given name first and the surname last, Mr Keijiro Watanabe. (For the pronunciation of Japanese, see Chapter 8, 'Hints for Visitors'.)

# 6

## *How They Get About*

THE Japanese are inveterate tourists. They love to travel. The roads were the scene of stir, bustle, life and colour in traditional Japan. Merchants went up and down the Tokaido, the east sea road, between the new capital of Edo (the modern Tokyo) and the old capital of the Emperor at Kyoto, and had a good time at the inns where they changed pack-horses or spent the night.

The roads were also the scene of strife and quarrels in spite of rigorous policing. The *daimyo*, or great lords, had perforce to travel from their country seats to the Shogun's capital at Edo to attend court on a rota system. They were accompanied on their journey by a large and impressive retinue of armed samurai, servants, porters, horses, palanquins and household goods. Everyone encountering such a procession was supposed to dismount and prostrate himself in the dust by the roadside out of respect. An Englishman in 1862 failed to do so, and was set upon by samurai of the Satsuma clan and killed. The British government demanded a ransom, and when it was not promptly forthcoming had the Royal Navy shell the Satsuma town of Kagoshima. So far from being incensed against the British for this, the Satsuma warriors decided to learn how to be equally efficient as a fighting force and sent some of their best men to England for naval training. This was the foundation of the Japanese Imperial Navy. But we are straying into history. (Those desiring further information on this period are referred to a book by this author, *Japan—Its History and Culture*, Thomas Y. Crowell Co, New York, 1970; to be published in England by David & Charles (Holdings) Limited in 1973.)

Many Japanese who were neither merchants nor lords travelled not because they had to but because they liked to. Since there was no category 'tourist' in the old days, these people would go on a pilgrimage. Genuine Buddhist religious motives were there, but often the motives of restlessness and curiosity were added, as with Chaucer's Canterbury pilgrims and others in medieval Europe. Japanese pilgrims came from all walks of life from the Emperor downwards, wore distinctive dress and often travelled long distances to remote shrines or mountain tops.

The modern Japanese are still tourists, and now they are going abroad in large numbers, a recent trend.

### RAILWAYS

The first Japanese railway was built in 1872, between Tokyo and the port of Yokohama, a distance of about 18 miles. It was an instant success and was carrying 2 million passengers by 1880, as well as large quantities of freight. The railway system is divided into a public and private sector. Japan National Railways operates by far the longer track mileage, 12,934 miles or four-fifths of the total. But 154 private companies operate urban railways, feeder lines, mountain railways and other routes used by tourists. As a result they carry 40 per cent more passengers per year than the national railways, but handle almost no freight.

The New Tokaido Line of the Japanese National Railways, dating from 1964, runs limited-stop super-express trains from Tokyo to Osaka, 320 miles in 3hr 10min. These trains are quiet and comfortable and attain a maximum speed of 130mph. The line was completely rebuilt, running in many parts on elevated tracks over streets and houses. The track consists of welded steel rail on rubber pad, and the whole is set in pre-stressed concrete. The train axles are individually powered, which gives extremely smooth operation.

Construction has begun on the New Sanyo Line from Osaka

to Fukuoka in the industrial area of northern Kyushu. Completion is expected in 1975, and the full distance from Tokyo to Fukuoka, 668 miles, will be covered in 6hr 40min with speeds up to 155mph.

Railway trains in Japan, though often crowded, are clean, efficient and punctual. If a commuter's train is more than a few minutes late, he receives a note of the fact to show to his firm. But when you travel on a Japanese train, be ready to get off promptly at your destination; the train may only halt at the station for one minute. You receive ample warning (in Japanese) on the train loudspeaker system. A courteous voice tells you when such and such a stop is coming and which side of the train to get off, asks you not to forget your parcels, and sometimes adds greetings suitable to the time of year.

The first monorail system was opened in 1964 to connect the airport to downtown Tokyo. Plans have been made for a 23 mile submarine tunnel to connect the northern island of Hokkaido to the main island by rail by the year 1975.

There are underground or subway systems in Tokyo, Osaka, Kobe and Nagoya. In spite of frequent trains the Tokyo underground is packed with passengers beyond belief. Special personnel are engaged to push people into trains so that the automatic doors will close. It is said that additional personnel had to be hired to act as 'pullers', to pull out passengers who had only succeeded in getting an arm or a leg into the doorway but could not force the rest of their bodies in. I have not actually seen these latter servants of the public at work, but I can readily believe in their existence.

## ROADS

The national government only took over the development of roads in 1964–5. Plans have been made for the construction of thirty-two national trunk routes totalling 4,720 miles by 1985. The expressway from Nagoya to Kobe was opened in 1965, and the stretch in the other direction from Nagoya to Tokyo in 1969. The various types of Japanese roads in 1968 were as follows:

| Table 10 Nature of road | Length in miles | Approximate percentage of road improved (width, curves, gradient) |
|---|---|---|
| National expressways | 389 | 100·0 |
| National highways | 18,126 | 81·4 |
| Prefectural roads | 78,112 | 27·2 |
| City, town and village roads | 532,771 | 14·0 |

Records reveal the difficult nature of the coastal terrain by showing for the 389 miles of national expressways the extraordinary total of 800 bridges (of 2¼yd length and upwards) and 31 tunnels.

### AUTOMOBILES

At this point one out of every eleven Japanese owns a car. About twice as many persons proportionately own cars in Britain, France and Germany. In the USA one person out of two owned a car as far back as 1966. The total number of automobiles in Japan in 1968, namely 4·29 million, represents a sharp increase over a mere 48,000 in 1950 and 1·89 million in 1965. Japan is now third in motor vehicle production behind USA and West Germany, having surpassed Britain in this respect. Japan produced 4,085,826 vehicles in 1968, as contrasted with almost 9 million manufactured in the USA. Out of 19 automobile makers in Japan, the top 5 in order of popularity at home are Toyota, Nissan (Datsun), Toyo Kogyo, Mitsubishi and Daibatsu Kogyo. Toyota and Nissan together have captured more than half the total market and are also the major exporters.

The number of cars exported has risen from 2 per cent of Japanese production in 1950 to 8 per cent in 1968. Almost one-sixth of the 360,000 motor vehicles exported by Japan in 1967 went to the USA. Japanese cars are much less commonly seen in Britain.

All Japanese cars are fairly small. One of the most popular cars on the domestic market, the two-cylinder, four-passenger Toyota Publica, costs only about £423 or $1,100. Delivery on most cars is about a week, with any kind of desired equipment, and some models come in 120 colours. Japanese owners are starting to turn their cars in regularly in order to buy new ones. A second car in the family has become a status symbol, but now this mark of status is being replaced by the ownership of a second home at the shore or in the country.

Buses are now used extensively in Japan, not so much for urban transport as for excursion and tourist purposes. They also act as feeder lines for railways in remote or mountainous regions, in which Japan abounds.

## SHIPPING

An indication of the importance of shipping to Japan is given by the fact that 40 per cent of domestic trade goods are carried by sea, 30 per cent by rail and 30 per cent by road. When Japan was closed to the outside world from the seventeenth century to the nineteenth, a limit was placed by law on the size of vessels which could be built, in order to make them suitable only for coastwise trade and unable to venture overseas. But very soon after Japan decided to modernise, the Nippon Yusen Kaisha (Japan Mail Line) grew up as an offshoot of the great Mitsubishi firm and began to conduct overseas trade in large ocean-going liners and cargo vessels, sailing from Kobe and Yokohama.

Japan profited by the war losses of British and American vessels in World War I and began to capture a large share of the Pacific and world carrying trade. Coming late into the competitive field and aiming always for the most recent technology, she was able to bypass to a great extent the age of the cumbrous reciprocating marine engine and proceed straight to steam-turbine propulsion.

The closing of the Suez Canal in the mid-1960s gave great impetus to the use of super-oil-tankers going by the long Cape route. Of the 69 vessels in the world over 100,000 tons in 1967, 57 were built in Japanese yards, for Japan had been planning large ships since 1954. The *Universe Ireland* oil-tanker has a tonnage of 312,000 and vessels of 500,000 tons are projected. Ships of this size are actually too large to pass through the Straits of Malacca, and this passage may be enlarged to accommodate them.

### AIRLINES

The main domestic carriers are Japan Air Lines (much the largest), All-Nippon Airways and Japan Domestic Air Lines. All overseas flights are operated by Japan Air Lines. Tokyo and Osaka have large international airports, and in addition there are 90 airfields for domestic flights.

The Japanese international service began in 1954 with the Tokyo/San Francisco route. In 1966 Japan Air Lines ran:

20 flights a month to USA and Canada
8            to Europe
29            to South-East Asia
and 5            to Korea

In 1967 a round-the-world service via New York was instituted, and a route to Moscow opened via Siberia in conjunction with Aeroflot. International services of Japan Air Lines have been greatly expanded—to 41 trips a week both ways across the Pacific—and in 1969 the line carried 1,314,279 passengers, more than double the figure for 1966. This line is now in eighth place among the member airlines of the International Air Transport Association.

There is just one problem—not enough flat land to put down big aircraft. Tokyo Airport was built on land reclaimed from Tokyo Bay.

# 7

# *How They Amuse Themselves*

THE Japanese, in common with the rest of mankind, find amusement in a myriad ways, according to personal choice. Emperor Hirohito makes marine biology his hobby; and one Japanese boy asked what the English word for *basuboru* was, thinking of baseball as a sport native to his country, so beloved is it of so many. Particularly popular are tourism, sport and theatre. In all of these the reader will notice a blending or co-existence of the old and the new.

### TOURISM

The Japanese are indefatigable tourists, and always have been. Emperors in the past visited temples, usually nearby, or held parties in the country to view the cherry trees in the spring or the maples in the autumn. Monks wandered to distant shrines on pilgrimage, and in the Edo Period (seventeenth to nineteenth centuries) there was constant coming and going of lords and their retinues, merchants and common folk on the roads by the sea shore and through the mountain passes. A famous series of coloured woodblock prints by the artist Hiroshige shows 53 post-stations and tourist views along the Tokaido, the east sea road from the old capital to the new.

The Japanese like to take the whole family to see the sights. On other occasions the children go off in school groups conducted by teachers to national shrines, such as the chief Shinto shrine at Ise or some of the famous temples of Kyoto.

Many of these tourists go by rail. Japan has the greatest

volume of railway passenger traffic in the world, 270,000 million passenger-kilometres in 1968, as compared to 22,500 million in the UK, and slightly less than the UK figure in the USA. Much of this enormous Japanese figure is attributable to daily commuter traffic, but tourism accounts for a sizeable proportion. Tourists also visit mountain resorts, hot-spring spas and national parks by numerous bus lines.

Buddhist temples and Shinto shrines, some of surpassing beauty, some with famous gardens, some more ordinary, form frequent objects of tourist trips. Religious motives are here mixed with a simple desire to see the sights in a happy-go-lucky combination typical of the sunny and naïve Japanese approach to folk-religion. Japanese temples indeed cater for all tastes. Devout worshippers bow and pray before impressive ancient images of Buddha, in whose faces the genius of bygone craftsmen has combined a detached calm and a tender compassion which defy description. But in the same temple you can buy a numbered piece of paper which tells your fortune; and in the crowded streets leading up to the temple on its wooded hillside are displayed all manner of fairings—small images, cheap china, food, coca-cola, and mass-produced souvenirs catering for the simple and vulgar tastes of tourists everywhere in the world.

---

A mammoth oil-tanker and other vessels in one of the efficiency-conscious Japanese shipyards. Ships now account for over 8 per cent of total exports, second only to steel.

Light industry continues to be an important factor in the Japanese economy. Large numbers of women are employed in the making of watches, cameras, textiles, radios, television sets and tape-recorders. The illustration shows watches in a water-proofing test.

Japanese tourists in these days of modern affluence have begun to turn to travel abroad. The US Embassy in Tokyo reports a spectacular rise in applications for visas for America every summer. Hawaii, Hong Kong and the Philippines are flooded with Japanese tourists, all of whom carry cameras. Trips to America are still undertaken mainly in groups under guides able to cope with the unfamiliar language and surroundings of the United States. The favourite itineraries cover the west coast and the great national parks, such as Yellowstone, with much less interest being shown in the far distant east coast. Japanese tourist travel to Europe has also markedly increased. In addition to the large group tours, individual Japanese of sophistication and experience are to be seen in ever larger numbers in the museums, concert halls, resorts and university centres of the world.

## SPORT

*Sumo*

Both traditional and Western sports are immensely popular in Japan. The scene of the *sumo* wrestling tournaments in Tokyo is a vast down-town arena, with much of the colour and

---

Japanese kimonos come in every colour of the rainbow. The young girls wear designs of more gaiety than the married women. The back part of the elaborate obi or sash is to be seen on the girl on the right. The wrap-around kimono as a dress for men and women is derived from medieval China.

To the Japanese, gardens are more than gardens—they are art, poetry and philosophy. This famous garden, in a style of classic simplicity influenced by Zen Buddhism, belongs to the Katsura Imperial Villa (or Detached Palace) in Kyoto.

G

life of eighteenth-century urban society still preserved. You are met by an attendant in the baggy trousers gathered at the knee and the short coat of the former artisan costume, who takes your tickets and looks after you very solicitously. You may want to look at the *sumo* museum with its costumes, fans, prints and other mementoes of champions of the past. Or, if very privileged, you may have an introduction to one of the recent champions, now retired, who act as judges. You will then be conducted behind the scenes near the dressing-rooms to a large tatami-mat room in which the great man holds court.

When the time draws near for the matches to begin, you will be taken to your reserved section of matting in the arena itself. Everything is done in traditional style; there is not a chair in the place. But there is plenty of diversion in addition to the tournament proper. Your attendant will bring you beer and sake, *sembei* or savoury biscuits, and later a complete Japanese meal. You will also be given an *omiage*, complimentary present of a blue and white porcelain jar and bowl to take away, although all these extras are no doubt reflected in the price of your ticket.

The centre of everyone's attention is the ring, a circular, padded platform raised on sacks of rice-straw, and surmounted above by its own separate roof in the style of a Shinto shrine. In fact the whole affair is steeped in Shinto ritual and feeling. The referee wears a formal costume and hat of priestly cut, and before each bout the two contestants throw a handful of salt into the ring, obviously the remnant of a purificatory rite. The sport is mentioned in the historical records as being known 2,000 years ago.

The proceedings open with the formal entry of the wrestlers and their parade round the ring. Their costume is minimal, consisting of a heavy, tightly knotted loincloth and an elaborate hair-do with a bun on top. For the parade they also wear a decorated apron and thick belt of twisted straw-rope. There is a pronounced sense of traditional mystique about the contest, in which the audience obviously share.

The minor bouts come first, and as the day wears on more

experienced wrestlers compete, until the culminating bouts of the champions and grand champions. The object is to make some part of the opponent's body, other than his feet, touch the ground, or else to force him out of the unfenced ring. The wrestlers, all professional, seem almost to be a special breed of men, taller than the average Japanese, immensely heavy and strong. Some are able to pick up their opponents bodily and hurl them to the ground. Since no opponent seems less than about 16 stone (or over 220lb), this is no mean feat.

The preliminaries to the bout have a certain fascination. Each wrestler, facing his opponent and glaring at him, squats and rises, flexes his muscles, and transfers his weight to one leg, raising the other high in the air to one side. This threat display, with no actual contact, is explained as necessary in order to summon up the required concentration and co-ordination of mind and body. Either contestant is entitled at this point to break off by turning away, and his opponent then may not attack him. Most take advantage of the full legal allotment of preliminary trials; but when the moment has come, battle is swiftly joined and the actual wrestling time is usually very brief before one vanquishes the other and is declared the winner. Sumo champions have a huge popular following when they take part in the six annual tournaments in the main cities.

## Judo

Judo, a specialised training in self-defence, has now become a sport of world-wide fame. The first international judo championship was held in Tokyo in 1956 and included entries from twenty-one countries. Judo is much more highly regarded in Japan than karate, which is gaining rapidly in popularity in the United States. Kendo, Japanese fencing, similar to the old English single-stick fighting, and kyudo, Japanese archery, are two other popular forms of those traditional martial arts which were widely practised in the Edo Period. At this time the samurai warriors had to keep in training, but found no outlet for their energies in actual warfare, either internal or external, during Japan's long period of isolation.

*Modern Sports*

Since Japan was host to the 18th Olympic Games in 1964, it is scarcely necessary to say that every form of Western athletics is carried on in Japan. Among the ninety-four countries competing in that year Japan won the third largest number of gold medals, after the United States and the Soviet Union. Sapporo in Hokkaido was the site of the 1972 Winter Olympics. The modern sports most popular in Japan are baseball, volleyball, table tennis and swimming. Next in order of popularity come rugby football, soccer, skiing, basketball and golf. As an indoor sport bowling (American style) has run like wildfire through the country.

Baseball is played by schoolchildren, college students, workers and professionals. Young men are to be seen in their lunch-break hurling a baseball back and forth for practice in narrow city lanes with complete abandon. There are two professional baseball leagues, the Central and the Pacific, each with six clubs, competing in regular games from April until October.

The Japanese table tennis team took five of the seven championship titles at Stockholm in 1957, and the women's volleyball team was victorious in Moscow in 1962.

Japanese businessmen increasingly take their recreation, and doubtless conclude some of their deals, on the 559 golf courses of Japan. These courses are carefully manicured and every stick and twig is picked up. Some are in most picturesque natural surroundings. The hard-working women of Japan act as caddies. Golf in Japan, however, as in America, tends to be a rich man's game. And so far Japanese professionals have not figured prominently in any of the great international golf tournaments.

Skiing has of late become a very popular sport, for which Japan has many excellent slopes available, although many of the best are somewhat remote from the centres of population.

Students and young people will think nothing of travelling all night by train for a couple of days' skiing at the week-end. There are estimated to be over 6 million skiers in the country, of whom 40 per cent are women. Mountain climbing is also extensively practised and Alpine clubs are increasing. In 1969 five Japanese men and one woman scaled the dreaded Eiger North Face in Switzerland, 3,974m, in what is claimed to be the first direct vertical ascent ever attempted.

### THEATRE

The theatre in Japan probably offers a wider variety of living forms, from classical Nō to night-club, than can be found anywhere else in the world. Perhaps this is because the Japanese are an artistic people and tend to express themselves in forms and conventions. Good theatre is not a photograph of life, which would be tediously dull; it is a heightened version of life, intensified by being compressed into a small space. The intensification is made by a rigid yet infinitely varied set of conventions. But when the playwrights and actors are complete masters of the forms, life and character flow freely through to the audience.

The stiffest and most archaic of the conventions are to be seen in the Nō plays, a form of drama put together in the fourteenth and fifteenth centuries by a father and son of genius, Kanami and Zeami, out of earlier elements of religious, aristocratic and popular drama. Everyone should see a Nō play at least once. The antique costumes are gorgeous with coloured silk brocade, and the masks—plain, oval and bland for a young woman, wrinkled for an old man, and grotesque with a flowing red wig for a demon—give an intentional sense of distance from everyday reality. The performance is a complex mixture of mime, posture-dance, chanting, speech and music, the last provided by a small orchestra of flute and drums, seated on stage. The gradually accelerating rhythm of the drums in moments of dramatic crisis creates an almost unbearable sense of tension. There is no scenery save the painting of a pine-tree at the rear of the stage.

The Nō plays, reflecting the Buddhist view of the world, deal with universal themes, the glory and sadness of war, love and jealousy, death and the spirit world. The element of plot is of small importance, since the story or legend is known in advance to the audience, as it was in classical Greek tragedy. The skill of writers and actors is seen in the way in which the character and emotions of the personages are portrayed as universal human experiences, belonging to a heroic realm that is larger than life. But where Greek tragedy relies on the clear verbal exposition of motive and character, Nō drama uses mime, stylised dance and chanting to suggest by subtle and indirect means the mood of the piece. The Greeks appeal to reason, even though the chorus dance out their emotions; the Japanese appeal to intuition, even though the actors use words.

Kabuki, the popular theatre of the townsmen of the eighteenth and nineteenth centuries, and still a living and favourite form of entertainment, is more direct than Nō in its blood-and-thunder presentation. It has more actors, a wider stage, more props, more 'spectacle', with acting and dialogue which is much nearer to the Western idea of drama, though still rich in conventions of a peculiarly Japanese kind. Kabuki takes its varied themes from legend and history, as does Nō, but adds a whole range of plays from ordinary life—even low life—in the towns. It revels in comedy situations with which its urban audience is familiar. There is the country bumpkin who is taken advantage of by the city slicker, but somehow gets his own back; and there is the stupid but fundamentally decent husband whose nagging wife receives her just deserts.

The early Kabuki companies of players consisted of both men and women. Their morals were considered to be more than a little shady, and so the authorities forbade women to act. (Nō companies also are exclusively male.) Women's parts then had to be taken by men, many of whom became extremely skilful and popular, devoting a lifetime to the study and portrayal of the most subtle female mannerisms.

Kabuki has been much affected by the style of Bunraku, the puppet theatre, famous playwrights such as Chikamatsu Monzaemon having composed plays for both. The puppeteers in Bunraku, clad in black, do not attempt to hide themselves from the audience, but such is their expertise in manipulating the large-size puppets and effacing themselves that after a short time one is scarcely aware of their presence at all.

## OTHER ENTERTAINMENT

When it comes to modern, Western forms of entertainment, Tokyo has in some shape or another all that any great city has to offer, regular plays, avant-garde theatre, cabaret shows and night-club entertainers. The famous Takarazuka all-girl troupe, modelled originally on the Rockettes chorus line in Radio City Music Hall, New York, puts on revues with precision and sparkle. There are several very good orchestras performing classical music in Japan, and concerts are often sold out. Jazz and rock music naturally enjoy a great vogue among young people.

Japanese films run the whole gamut from sensitive masterpieces of subtle photographic understatement to the crudest type of sex- and violence-orientated pictures, many of the latter directed towards a teenage audience. The film industry is large and flourishing, and carries on a considerable export trade. Nevertheless, domestic attendance in theatres suffers, in Japan as elsewhere, from television competition. Television sets are in practically every home.

## RESTAURANTS

The restaurants of Japan deserve a volume to themselves. More Japanese families and young people 'eat out' than ever in the past. And they have the utmost variety to choose from. The large cities have restaurants with quite passable German,

French, Italian and Chinese food. There are small Japanese restaurants and large ones, of every standard and price. Some of the expensive restaurants have delightful Japanese rooms or alcoves for private parties, with tatami mats and tasteful décor. Others have plain benches and tables, with cheap but nourishing food. Foreigners seeking Japanese food generally prefer either *tempura* or *sukiyaki*. (In the latter word the u is almost silent, 's'kiyaki'.) *Tempura* consists of shrimp and pieces of vegetable fried crisp in deep fat, and is simply delicious. Since the Japanese also like *tempura*, choose a restaurant patronised by Japanese, with no English-language signs: those restaurants designed for foreigners tend to be long on vegetable and short on shrimp, as well as high in price. The name *tempura* is said to have originated in 'quattuor tempora', the 'four times' a year when the sixteenth-century Jesuits in Japan could not eat meat and turned to sea-food. *Sukiyaki* is a dish of thin slices of beef and various vegetables cooked in an iron pan in front of the guests. Each piping-hot bite is dipped in raw egg before being eaten. An expensive delicacy is Kobe beef, from steers which are said to be nourished on beer and massaged daily to make their meat tender. Most Westerners avoid *sashimi*, raw fish, but it really tastes very good, if you like exotic flavours and the strong sauces which sometimes go with it.

The more exclusive Japanese restaurants specialise not only in their food but in a recherché atmosphere of refinement and privacy. Businessmen patronising them often add to their expense accounts an item for *geisha*, the hostesses for which Japan is famous. Since the place of the Japanese wife has for so long been in the seclusion of the home, men have sought women of another type to entertain them in public, to break the ice of social convention—thicker in Japan than elsewhere, to pour their saké liquor, to sing, dance, play the samisen, and generally make conversation, running from literary allusions to light repartee or broad and bawdy humour. Certain of the most famous geisha command high prices and are strict in the observance of their own conventions. Others become the mistresses of wealthy men, and still others are not very different from prostitutes, though this is not true of the profession of geisha as a whole. The Kyoto New Year procession of geisha and their *maiko*, or maids, all dressed in bright kimonos and obi, or sashes, is one of the sights of Japan.

The cafés of Japan have developed in a manner peculiarly their own. They are in origin completely foreign, and vary from tea- or coffee-shops, where cakes and pastries are served, to bars and taverns, with or without hostesses. The coffee-shops are frequented by students, young people, often in couples, and ladies out shopping. Businessmen and young men-about-town frequent the 'cafés', which are really bars. The hostesses in them dress in the Western manner, but behave as geisha whose speciality is the light entertainment of men. Since the threshold of Japanese tolerance of alcohol tends to be low, café and certain restaurant parties often become raucous and rowdy. It is said that the Japanese tendency to get drunk easily is due to the lack of fat in the national diet. But for one noisy bar one can find a dozen quiet Japanese restaurants where, increasingly, father takes the whole family to dine out.

LITERATURE

*Poetry*

An ingenious scholar has come up with a correlation between milk and epic poetry, namely that no epic poetry has appeared among nations such as China and Japan which do not go in for drinking milk. No one has ventured to put forward a reason for this curious piece of information. It is, however, a fact that Japanese poems have always been short, portraying a mood rather than a series of events, a feeling rather than a sustained dramatic sequence. An early collection of poetry, the *Manyoshu* ('Collection of a Myriad Leaves'), compiled in the mid-eighth century, is of this type, using symbols from nature to call forth a mood with an admirable economy of words. Among the thousands of poems in the collection themes such as love, sadness at banishment, the evanescence of human happiness, and

affection for the countryside and familiar life of Japan recur
frequently.

Some of the poems in the Myriad Leaves collection consist
of only thirty-one syllables. But the culmination of brevity was
reached in a later form of verse, the *haiku*, which tells its whole
story in seventeen syllables, arranged in lines of 5–7–5. *Haiku*
are poems of nimble wit, arising from the bourgeoisie and the
'cockney' urban milieu of the seventeenth century. The best
known *haiku* author is Matsuo Basho, who lived in the latter
half of the seventeenth century and was thus a contemporary
of Herrick, Racine and Molière. But the form continues to be
popular right down to the present day in Japan, and is now
catching on abroad.

The *haiku* may be said to be a vignette, the fragment of a
natural scene, and then a quick, subjective twist showing, or
just hinting, how the scene or incident affects the poet himself.
When the form originally became popular, it did so because
it had a certain frivolous cheekiness, which poked fun, often
by implication, at the solemnities of aristocratic and feudal
circles. The *haiku* is slight, and makes the most of slight subjects; but that does not preclude, in the hands of a master, a
refreshing honesty, a touch of profound philosophy, or a charming pathos.

Here are a few examples of *haiku*, the first four by Basho:

The Unknown Flower
*To bird and butterfly*
*unknown, a flower blooms—*
*the autumn sky.*

(Basho)

The 'Inn of the World'
*At this same inn*
*slept pleasure women too,*
*bush-clover and the moon!*

(Basho)

### A Wish

*I'd like enough drinks*
*to put me to sleep—on stones*
*covered with pinks.*

(Basho)

### Death Poem of Basho, taken ill on a journey

*On a journey, ill*
*and over the fields, all withered, dreams*
*go wandering still.*

(Basho)

### The Wild Geese Leave

*Wild geese! I know*
*that they did eat the barley;*
*yet, when they go . . .*

(Yasui)

### The Little Duck

*'I've just come from a place*
*at the lake bottom!'*—that *is the look*
*on the little duck's face.*

(Jōsō)

### The Courtesan's Prayer

*If of love I die,*
*then above my grave-mound,*
*cuckoo—come and cry!*

(Oshu, late eighteenth-century courtesan)

### The Snail

*Snail, my little man,*
*slowly, oh, very slowly*
*climb up Fujisan!* [Mt Fuji]

(Issa)

(All the above poems are translated by Harold G. Henderson, and are to be found in his excellent book, *An Introduction to Haiku*, Doubleday, Garden City, New York, 1958.)

Part of the appeal of the *haiku* to modern man in Japan and the West is that it is open-ended, leaving the question undecided, appealing for the co-operation of the reader's imagination. Since the poet cannot possibly do more in seventeen syllables than hint at a meaning, the reader has to apply the image of the poem and complete the picture and its significance in his own mind. Many who feel that in the past poetry has been too didactic or too precious or too supercharged emotionally, and that modern poetry is too obscure and experimental even to make sense, enjoy *haiku* because these verses are light and casual. They do have a point, even perhaps a moral, but they include the reader on a take-it-or-leave-it basis.

The popularity of short poems in Japan today may be judged from the fact that each New Year the Emperor holds a poetry competition, in which he and members of the imperial family contribute brief poems. Thousands are sent in from all over the nation, and prizes awarded for the best.


*Prose*

Prose literature has been highly valued in traditional Japan. The *Tale of Genji*, written by a court lady about AD 1000, is one of the great novels of the world. It is the story of the loves of a handsome prince, and treats with charm and insight the universal themes of love, death and art in the rather precious setting of the Heian court of the author's time.

This aristocratic literature was succeeded by warrior romances in Japan's medieval period. These stirring tales of loyalty amid the seesaw of victory and defeat have been the source of plot and character for numerous plays, both in the classical Nō drama and the more popular Kabuki, and now in modern films which correspond to our Westerns. The romances are usually written from the point of view of one family or clan.

They delight in braggadocio, colour, pageantry and the description of stratagems and battles.

*Borne at last on the shoulders of white-robed priests, and shimmering blindingly with encrustments of gold, slowly, slowly swaying, the Sacred Shrine made its way down the hill on to the great highway.*

*A figure suddenly darted out in front of the oncoming shrine and held up a hand. 'Wait, you infernal priests!' On his head was a black helmet of iron, bare of insignia; he was incased in black armour, wore straw sandals, and held up a long bow. Not far behind him were Tokitada and Heiroku, unarmed, their faces set like hard masks.*

*'I, Lord Aki, Kiyomori of the Heiké, demand that you hear me. Among all you evil ones there must be at least one who will listen to reason.'*

*To the advancing host he looked like Asura, the God of War, hewn out of jet, with yawning jaws from which issued a torrent of sound.*

*Astounded by the temerity of this fellow and his words, the monks shouted: 'Whew! . . . Kiyomori!' Then a mad roaring broke loose. 'Slash him to bits for the festival of blood!'*

*The Shrine-bearers pushed back the angry crowd, crying: 'No man shall come near the Shrine and defile it! Beware of the sacred emblem!'*

. . . . .

*Consternation spread through the monks as Kiyomori fitted an arrow to his bow; it creaked as he arched it like the full moon; then he aimed straight at the Shrine.*

*One of the leaders leaped forward shrieking: 'Alas! a curse on you, blasphemer! You shall die foaming blood!'*

*'Die? Then so be it.'*

*The bowstring twanged, the arrow hissed and pierced the very centre of the Shrine. From two thousand throats came a frenzied roar.*

The above extract comes, not from an old book, but from a best-selling historical novel, *The Heiké Story*, written in 1951 by Eiji Yoshikawa (English translation by Uramatsu, Knopf, New York, 1956), and based on the famous medieval romance, *Heike Monogatari*. Despite their emphasis on violence, these romantic tales are suffused with the true Buddhist sense of the spiritual which is reflected in the opening sentences of the original *Heike Monogatari*:

> *The temple bell echoes the impermanence of all things. The colours of the flowers testify to the truth that those who flourish must decay. Pride lasts but a little while, like a dream on a spring night. Before long the mighty are cast down, and they are as dust before the wind.*

Two remaining types of prose literature may be briefly mentioned, the genre literature of urban life, sometimes low life, in the seventeenth and eighteenth centuries, and the contemporary Japanese novel. Typical of the first is the collection of short stories by Ihara Saikaku entitled *Five Women who Loved Love*. Here is a new realism, centred not, as were the old romances, on the noble and the warrior, but, like the *haiku*, on the ordinary man. The literature of urban life revolves around the merchant, the young man about town, who takes his ease in the teahouses and places where he can meet a girl in the pleasure quarters of Edo. The characters are smart and pert and sometimes pathetic, but always very human. The stories of actors, prostitutes, merchants, wastrels and masterless samurai warriors who have wandered into town reflect 'the floating world', the world of the pleasure of the moment, which is also portrayed in the famous Japanese woodblock colour prints of about the same period.

Among contemporary writers the most distinguished is Kawabata, who was awarded the Nobel prize for literature, the first Asian novelist to have received this honour. The works of Yukio Mishima, however, are more popular. He was a prolific author and a master literary craftsman. His recent suicide, committed as a gesture to recall his country to her traditional warrior values of loyalty, courage and the disciplined life, drew attention to his complex personality, at once Japanese and Western. In spite of his passionate love of Japan, his house was filled with furniture and art objects from the West. One of his short novels which has had a wide appeal is *The Sound of Waves*, the story of an island, its fishermen and the innocent tenderness of young people in love. The narration is spare and disarmingly simple, but the story well reflects the conflict of values in modern Japan.

There are 14,000 bookstores in Japan. Since the whole country is only the size of California, this translates itself into a bookstore in nearly every village and one every few blocks in the large cities. The Japanese read avidly, during lunch-hour, on trains and buses, in the park, whenever they get a chance.

Although the bookstores are crowded, it is surprising to find that there are comparatively few public libraries, certainly less than in most Western countries. The National Diet Library, on the other hand, is a large institution, corresponding to the Library of Congress. In addition to the main library in Tokyo, it has branches in five cities and in thirty government agencies, and possesses between 5 and 6 million volumes.

### ART

In art, as in most matters, the Japanese are right up to date. They have made notable contributions in the field of contemporary and abstract art, in painting and sculpture, and have had works shown in many world exhibitions and galleries of international repute.

Of all forms of Western art, classical music probably makes the greatest appeal to Japanese. There are several symphony orchestras in Japan, and concerts are frequently sold out. Classical records find a ready sale. Japan is now launching on the international concert circuit some instrumentalists and conductors of the first rank. Jazz and popular Western music also enjoy a great vogue.

There is now a fairly vigorous two-way traffic in design and taste. Western architectural and industrial product design imported into Japan, though previously of a rather poor quality, is now becoming much more sophisticated and pleasing. In the other direction Japanese design in furniture, gardens and architecture is distinctly affecting the West. The Japanese long ago learned the value of simplicity and clean lines. They are adepts at the use of natural materials—stone, wood, bamboo, thatch—often untreated and unpainted. They value texture as much as shape and colour; and in this respect particularly their architects and craftsmen have contributed to the improvement of international taste.

Consciously seeking the new, even the latest, the Japanese nevertheless know the value of ancient forms in art and have conserved them. This fertilising effect of traditional forms upon modern art and design is not susceptible of explanation in a few words, but must be felt and experienced through a study of Japan's cultural past. Here it will be sufficient to indicate one or two areas in which the art of the past is very much alive in the present day, and forms a source of enjoyment and inspiration for many contemporary Japanese. The following forms of art appreciation and artistic endeavour are, it should be stressed, not exercises in archaism but very much a part of how the Japanese of a certain level live today. These conservative but energetic people are nourished and sustained by a sense of their own past to a degree rarely found elsewhere.

The most highly regarded art has long been that of landscape painting, an inheritance from the Chinese cultural tradition. The Sung Dynasty masters deeply affected such painters as Sesshu (1420–1506) in the Muromachi golden age of Japanese art. Yet Sesshu developed his own individual styles of impressionism, in one direction by hard, angular hatchet-strokes, and in the other by masses of black ink with soft edges in a form known as 'flung-ink' style. He was powerfully influenced by the philosophy of Zen Buddhism. In addition to landscapes, paintings of birds, flowers, insects and sea-creatures have also long been favourite subjects in the Chinese classical tradition beloved by the Japanese.

The popular, bourgeois art of urban life, which flourished strongly from the late seventeenth to the early nineteenth centuries, shows a complete contrast of subject and treatment, but comparable high standards of design and execution. This was the great age of the wood-block colour print, known as *ukiyo-e*, 'pictures of the floating world', a term derived from Buddhism and meaning the fleeting world of pleasure. Here the subjects are famous actors, popular geisha, beauties of the Yoshiwara pleasure district of Edo (Tokyo), and scenes of everyday life. Landscape is also treated, but in a more familiar manner, with plenty of colour and incident. The contemporary art of wood-block printing in Japan has been considerably influenced by the earlier prints. In the late nineteenth century these older prints came as a stimulating new experience to Toulouse-Lautrec and his contemporaries in France.

Since many of these prints could be produced from one set of blocks, their price was within the range of the ordinary townsman. And since they are easier than classical art for Westerners to understand and appreciate, they early became collectors' items in the West. Some were brought to Britain and the United States by the captains of clipper sailing-ships. The artist Utamaro is noted for his prints of willowy beauties, Hiroshige for his landscape series such as 'The Fifty-Three Stations of the Tokaido', Sharaku for his pictures of actors, and Hokusai both for landscapes and for a fund of inventive humour, deriving amusement from the whole human scene.

The Japanese are lovers of the *tour de force*, of the extreme in one form or another. Restrained as they are by form and politeness, the *tour de force* is a form of release, of humour and denial of convention. Hence the Japanese have cherished anecdotes of this type about men like Hokusai. He is reputed on one occasion to have used ink in a barrel and a broom for an artist's brush, tearing around a courtyard to finish a huge painting in a few minutes. No one could make anything of the

H

picture until one man had the idea of climbing to the roof of the nearby temple, when he saw that the drawing represented the face of the Buddhist saint, Daruma. Each eye had room for a man to sit down, and the mouth was as large as a gate. On another occasion Hokusai showed himself master of the small as well as the great by painting a picture of two sparrows on a single grain of rice. The Shogun Ienari held an artists' competition, and Hokusai won the prize in the following original manner. Asking for a paper screen door, he laid it flat and painted a wide, curving stripe of blue upon it. He then took a cock, dipped its feet in scarlet paint, and made it walk down the blue band. The title of the completed picture was, 'Maple Leaves Floating down the Tatsuta River'.

Traditional music is still very much alive in Japan, in the *fue* or flute, in the *samisen* or banjo-like instrument, in the *koto*, or long, rectangular, classical stringed instrument similar to a zither, and in the music of the theatre, with flute and drums.

Another form of living art is to be seen in *kado*, flower arrangement, of which there are several schools with differing traditions. Some stress mystical symbolism, in positions and levels of flowers in the arrangement corresponding to heaven, earth and man. Lacquer, silk brocades (for which Kyoto is famous), pottery and porcelain are still extensively manufactured by hand. I saw in the studio of a pottery artist in Hagi examples of bowls and cups made by thirteen generations of his ancestors, who came originally from Korea. As I sat in the room at the edge of a carp-filled pond, sipping tea, two modern Japanese businessmen came with their wives and concluded deals for the purchase of very expensive hand-made bowls of simple, even rough, but exquisite appearance for use in the tea-ceremony.

### THE PRESS

'The Press and all other forms of expression are guaranteed. No Censorship shall be maintained.' Thus Article 21 of the new Constitution seeks to insure that there shall be a free Press, unintimidated by the government. There have, however, been instances of journalists being imprisoned for refusing to reveal their sources of news items. The Nihon Shimbun Kyokai (Japan Newspaper Publishers' & Editors' Association), a voluntary society of great influence, has done much to maintain the standards of the Press and protect its liberty. Although the government respects the freedom of the Press, it must be admitted that big business exercises powerful leverage through control of advertising revenue.

The total circulation of newspapers in Japan is the third largest in the world, after the USSR and the USA. In circulation per head of the population Japan comes second in the world after Sweden. The three largest newspapers are the *Asahi Shimbun* with a combined circulation of all editions of 5·5 million, the *Yomiuri Shimbun* with 5·2 million and the *Mainichi Shimbun* with 4·7 million. There are two strong financial papers, the *Nihon Keizai Shimbun* and the *Sankei Shimbun*, each with about 2 million circulation. Together these five account for more than half the total circulation in the country. There are no less than 111 principal dailies with circulation over 50,000, including the English language press. Of the above number 28 are Tokyo papers. There are no newspaper chains. Each of the large dailies produces weekly and monthly periodicals. They also run radio and television broadcasting stations, as well as a number of other business undertakings. Some of these take the form of public service and enhance the paper's prestige; some are run for profit.

The Japanese Press is technically very advanced. Simultaneous editions are published in major cities, reproduced by high-speed radio photo-facsimile offset printing. Colour printing is generally of good quality. Teletype-setting was introduced by one firm in 1960, using a teleprinter for Chinese ideograms which was invented in Japan.

## BROADCASTING

Radio broadcasting began in Japan in 1925, and the NHK remained a monopoly until 1950, when private radio stations were authorised. The NHK is similar to the BBC in being a government-sponsored but largely independent organisation, and thus differs from the commercial radio stations under private enterprise in the USA. Television arrived on the scene in 1953, and immediately began expanding at a great rate. NHK operates 1,145 TV stations, and 62 private companies operate another 419 stations on a commercial basis, with advertising and singing commercials. To support the national broadcasting system each household with a radio or TV set registers and pays a fee. The NHK network must by law devote a high proportion of its time to cultural improvement, and the percentage of time given to different types of programme is as follows:

*Table 11*

| NHK TV | 1st Network | 2nd and 3rd Networks |
|---|---|---|
|  | % | % |
| News | 28·5 | 2·2 |
| Entertainment | 25·7 | 0·0 |
| Education | 9·9 | 81·2 |
| Cultural features | 35·9 | 16·6 |
| Daily air time in hours | 19·0 | 12·0 |

(Source: *Area Handbook for Japan: 1969*, US Government Printing Office)

Almost all TV stations in Japan broadcast regularly in colour, and about 90 per cent of local telecasts are composed of programmes based on Tokyo.

# 8

## *The Japanese and Other Peoples*

WE have been concerned thus far with what the present-day Japanese are really like and with how they manage their lives and their national affairs. But how did they come to be what they are?

They formed their new nation in conscious interaction with the rest of the world. They had isolated themselves for over two hundred years, from the early 1600s to the mid-1800s, just at the time when a great many exciting developments were taking place in the Western world, such as the rise of science, the American and French Revolutions and the foundations of the British Empire. Then quite suddenly in the late 1800s the Japanese deliberately decided to propel themselves into the midst of the modern world. The combination of a late start and a conscious decision to modernise meant that they were affected more than most nations by the various relationships with other peoples into which they entered. The Japanese also have a penchant for the latest international fashion, and this makes their relations with other peoples even more variable, delicate and crucial.

The British are said to have acquired their empire in a fit of absence of mind. In those early days they did not mind what others thought of them. Even today the remnants of an un-conscious, though perhaps ill-founded, sense of superiority are still to be seen in the country which defines its navy as the Royal Navy without thinking it necessary to specify to which sovereign this navy belongs. But not so with the Japanese. They are abnormally aware of the opinions of others. Their sensitive antennae are picking up messages all the time from everywhere. They are a constant puzzle to others, nourishing their own thoughts and their very special way of life—and yet aware of others, imitating, catching hold of ideas, adapting, choosing, adopting, rejecting; living their own lives but living them in a constantly varying international context.

This is not the place for a formal review of foreign policy; but a concluding glance at the attractions, repulsions and reactions the Japanese have felt in their encounters with other peoples of the world may perhaps be of value.

### THE FRENCH

In the early days of modernisation, before and after the Meiji Restoration of 1868, the Japanese sent missions abroad in order to discover which Western institutions would be best adapted to their needs. Many of their first models were French —the army, the administration of the educational system and elements of the Code Napoléon in law. A French legal expert, Gustave-Émile Boissonade, was chosen to assist the Japanese committee which worked out the new civil law code.

The connection between the French and the Japanese was, however, a two-way street, with artistic influences flowing in the opposite direction. The artist Degas, who affected the work of Gaugin, Toulouse-Lautrec and Picasso, was a great admirer of Japanese woodblock colour prints. Toulouse-Lautrec was a keen collector of such prints; and it has been said that, apart from Nature herself, Japanese prints were one of the deepest inspirations in the art of Van Gogh, who spent much of his short life in France. Gaugin's bold use of reds and yellows is thought to have stemmed from his admiration of this art form. The genre themes of Japanese prints, their charming portrayal of the life of the common people, their skilful and sweeping lines, their strong use of colour, and a theatrical exaggeration stopping just short of caricature, all came as a revelation to the searching and adventurous spirits of this famous group of French artists.

A fruitful cultural exchange continues. The Maison Franco-Japonaise in Kyoto is more effective in its work than most government-sponsored institutions of this type. And in general the Japanese admire French style in design, haute couture, jewelry and the world of the chic. The more sophisticated Japanese keep up with the latest trends in French art and literature. The French for their part appreciate Japanese subtlety, passion for modernity and the refined and impeccable taste exhibited in the best of Japanese art, both traditional and contemporary.

### THE BRITISH

At the time when the French in Japan were supporting the long legitimated but somewhat unpopular rule of the Tokugawa shoguns, the British Minister, Sir Harry Parkes, was backing the other side. This minor incident was typical of the eighteenth and nineteenth centuries: the British and French on opposite sides in North America and in India, in the intrigues and quarrels of the Nawabs of the Carnatic and Bengal, of the Sultans of Mysore and many others. So it was in Japan, with the difference that the Japanese settled the outcome of their own quarrels. Typically, however, it was the British Minister who guessed correctly in supporting the rebels of Satsuma and Choshu, who became the fiery young leaders and finally the Elder Statesmen of the Meiji Restoration.

A dramatic step forward in British-Japanese relations took place after 1862. It had an unexpected twist, for it started with a murder and flourished after a British bombardment. An Englishman, Charles Richardson, had refused to dismount from his horse when passing the procession of samurai warriors belonging to the Lord of Satsuma, and had been set upon and killed. When the fine demanded from Satsuma was not forthcoming, seven British ships bombarded the capital of the fief at

Kagoshima. Instead of the bitter resentment this action might have been expected to produce, the Japanese displayed admiration of the power and efficiency of the Royal Navy. Samurai from Satsuma were subsequently sent as naval cadets for training in Britain and purchases made in British shipyards. Close imitation of the practices and traditions of the Royal Navy formed the foundation of the Imperial Japanese Navy.

The navy was the decisive weapon in the growth of Japan's imperial power as seen in the war with China in 1894–5, when it inflicted a severe defeat on a more numerous but less well-trained Chinese fleet off the mouth of the Yalu River in north Korea. The strength of the navy proved even more decisive in the Russo-Japanese War of 1904–5. At this time Russia was viewed as a threat in Europe and there was alarm at her drive to the east across Siberia. Thus there was a good deal of sympathy with the plucky little Japanese who had dared to bait the great Russian bear in the fashionable but dangerous games of empire and war. By land the honours were even; at sea Japanese determination, skill and efficiency decided the outcome. When the Japanese actually won the war, it came as a shock. This was the first time an Oriental power had defeated a European one. It was a portent, and caused no little alarm among the established powers.

The British derived some satisfaction from the triumph of the Japanese navy men they had trained. To the Japanese the Anglo-Japanese Alliance, which ran from 1902 and was renewed in 1911, brought not only strategic but a certain emotional security, since Great Britain was then the dominant naval power in the world.

Japan's special relationship with the United Kingdom suffered a change after World War I, when the Anglo-Japanese Alliance gave place to a broader agreement negotiated at the Washington Conference of 1922. But despite surface shifts in policy, historians have noted that similar geographic positions have led to parallel developments in the history of Japan and Britain. Both are island nations lying off a great continental land-mass, each near enough to receive cultural influences from the continent, yet far enough away to derive some protection from the intervening waters. Both have gained a substantial portion of their livelihood from fishing, and have found in their hardy and experienced fishermen recruits for their navies. Both have seen their early pirates develop into merchant-adventurers; and some from other nations would describe the astute business men of each in the present day as being in the same continuing line of descent.

Japan has recently been able to raise sufficient rice to feed her population; but to pay for the imports of essential raw materials she must depend, as does Britain, on a high export volume of manufactured goods. Much of Japan's early machinery and many of the foreign advisers on technical matters came from British industry. In both countries also the degree of sophistication in the manufactures offered to overseas customers has had perforce to rise. Other countries are now making their own steel, textiles and simpler machinery, while Britain and Japan have moved on to precision tools, automobiles and electronic equipment. In the contemporary industrial race Japan has now outstripped Great Britain in many fields, particularly in that of shipbuilding.

### THE GERMANS

Ultimately, in the final reckoning, it may be found that the German influence was the most decisive of all at the time when Japan was doing her international shopping for ideas and institutions in the nineteenth century. One of the most important delegations was that sent abroad in 1882 under the leadership of Ito Hirobumi (later Prince Ito) in search of material for a national constitution. Ito paid visits to Washington and London, but spent most time where he had already decided he would find what Japan needed, namely in Berlin, at which point he met Bismarck, and in Vienna, where he was advised by Lorenz von Stein. The resulting Constitution, which came into force in 1889, gave large powers to the Emperor and to the oligarchy which formed the effective government. It also placed the army and the navy, in subsequent effect if not in theory, above and not under the civil authority.

German elements were introduced into the law code before its final promulgation. Yamagata Aritomo, sometimes styled 'the father of the Japanese Army', made important changes when he introduced the German general staff organisation. German doctors were brought to Japan to give instruction in medical schools; and until recently most Japanese doctors had to be able to do a large part of their reading in the German language.

It is not only in details of law and medicine that parallels with Germany are to be seen. In matters more inward—in a willingness to submit to discipline, in a certain thoroughness amounting at times to rigidity, in an insistence on 'going by the book' and by the letter of the law—the Japanese seem to exhibit traits very similar to those associated with the Prussians, though there is not necessarily any causal connection.


### THE AMERICANS

At a time too far back in history for the purposes of this book, the Japanese had become acquainted successively with the Koreans, the Chinese and the Mongols from their own part of the world, and then, in this order, with the Portuguese, the Spanish and the Dutch from distant Europe. Only the contact with the Dutch was long maintained, and that under strict controls.

But ideas are hard to control, and the undercover dissemination of Western learning had been gradually eroding Japan's isolationism from the late seventeenth century to the middle of the 19th. Just at the time when this and other factors were preparing Japan internally for a major change of direction, two great economic and cultural thrusts were gathering force elsewhere; the Russians were driving eastwards and the Americans as powerfully westwards.

The Americans, shut out from trade with Europe by mercantile laws, had shifted their attention to the Pacific, even though this meant rounding Cape Horn. Already in 1785 the ship *The Empress of China* had returned to New York after a successful trading voyage to China. A profitable three-cornered trade developed, manufactured goods being exchanged for furs in the Pacific north-west of America, and furs exchanged for Chinese luxuries such as tea and silk in Canton. Whaling and sealing then came to the fore as mercantile activities, and by 1846 America had 700 ships engaged in whaling, most of them in the Pacific.

China had experienced the impact of British economic ambitions in the Opium Wars of 1839–42. Japan was to feel the force of an American thrust, reaching her shores just ahead of the Russians, who had similar designs. President Fillmore's instructions to Commodore Matthew Perry of the United States Navy placed in the forefront a demand for better treatment of shipwrecked or distressed US sailors, but the President was ultimately more concerned to secure an opening for trade with Japan. The Americans meant business, and the Japanese closest to the negotiations realised this fact. Perry's instructions were to use persuasion and, if this failed, to employ 'more vigorous methods'. When the trade concession was reluctantly granted in 1854, other nations quickly followed the American lead and secured similar privileges. The most popular of the gifts presented by Commodore Perry to the Japanese at the celebrations which followed the signing of the treaty were significant—an electric telegraph, a small-scale railway and cases of whisky.

When modernisation was in full swing, however, America's main contribution seems to have been in the sphere of education. The early French-model school system became more liberal under American influence, and the six-year stay in Japan of Dr David Murray of Rutgers University, New Jersey, had a considerable effect on Japanese educational thinking. American missionary societies set high standards at all levels and pioneered education for girls.

Yukichi Fukuzawa, the Japanese who did more than any

other to popularise Western ideas, was greatly influenced by America. He spent some time in the United States in 1860 and in Europe in 1962. His immensely popular books, *Conditions in the West* and *Encouragement of Learning*, satisfied the curiosity of the average Japanese concerning ordinary life and social customs in the Western world. The school founded by Fukuzawa developed into Keio University, the first private university in Japan and still one of the best. The ideals of equality and freedom which Fukuzawa and others saw exemplified in the lives of George Washington and Abraham Lincoln made a powerful appeal to the Japanese reformers of this age, as they have to reformers in many countries at the time they have been casting off the shackles of a feudal past.

Coming nearer to the present day, we find that the relationship of the Japanese to Americans takes on a special love-hate character. The Japanese in their two thousand year history had never, up to World War II, suffered defeat combined with invasion of their sacred soil. The American post-war occupation could therefore have become a major disaster; instead it turned out to be, in most respects, a surprising success. At first the Japanese were full of fear. Women were advised by their relatives to leave town in case they suffered untold indignities. Looting and acts of revenge were expected to be widespread. When the American troops on the contrary proved to be not only well behaved but friendly, a wave of relief spread over the land. Fear turned to gratitude. Japanese hard work combined with American aid before long transformed an economic wasteland into a booming centre of production. The occupation emerged as one of the best planned and administered in military history. The formation of trade unions, a more liberal spirit in education and full participation in the democratic process were encouraged by the occupation authorities.

Inevitably in the course of time the early enthusiasm of the Japanese gave way to boredom as the period of occupation lengthened, and this in turn was succeeded by a predictable feeling of mild resentment. The Communist Party, though never strongly represented in the Diet, expanded its influence over students and intellectuals, and American policy began to play into its hands. Seen from a Western geopolitical point of view, some change in US policy was bound to occur after 1949, when the Chinese Communist Party took over the government of that country, and still more when the Korean War broke out in 1950. Security measures in Japan were tightened and the United States began to encourage the strengthening of Japan's self-defence forces in spite of the famous Article IX of the post-war Constitution renouncing war. Resentment at what seemed a cynical change of US policy was fostered by the leftist elements in Japanese political life. Ultimately in 1960 the Zengakuren, a student federation to the left even of the Communist Party, provoked demonstrations of such violence that the projected visit of President Eisenhower to Tokyo had to be cancelled and the Kishi government was forced to resign. Even in this extreme case, however, resentment was directed more against the Japanese establishment and its ties with America than against Americans themselves.

In the ups and downs of Japanese politics there is a tendency to lose sight of one primary fact—that the Japanese decided to throw in their lot with free enterprise and the free world of Western Europe and the United States. After World War II they were disillusioned with their own military leaders and the morass into which these men had led their nation. The people wholeheartedly rejected Fascism. But on the other hand they were not in the least inclined to accept Communism. The predominant complexion of every Diet and Cabinet since World War II has been conservative and capitalist. Liberal ideas have had a wide appeal and have been promoted by the political left partly as a means to discredit the government. (American ideas immediately after the war were liberal in contrast to those of the former Japanese military regime, but they now appear as conservative in contrast to the liberal opposition in Japanese politics.) Yet the responsible authorities in power have steadily maintained friendship with America and support of American policies as the only realistic road for Japan to travel. In the last few years there are signs that Japan, launched now with phenomenal success on the way of free enterprise, will exercise more independent leadership in foreign policy and develop her own stance in the world with or without the support of the United States.

## THE RUSSIANS

It is easier for a Japanese to be friendly with an Englishman or an American who is far away than with a Russian who is removed by only a short stretch of water. This is particularly true in the modern world of airpower, when the Japanese heartland is within easy reach of Russian bombers based in Siberia, but the Russian heartland is safely removed by thousands of miles behind the Ural Mountains.

Russian contacts with the Japanese began early. There were Russians in the Sea of Okhotsk by 1639, and a hundred years later a Russian vessel is known to have put in at ports on the east coast of Japan. In 1792 a Lieutenant Laxman was sent to Japan by the Governor of Siberia. When he arrived under guard at Matsumae there were parleys and feasts, but he was told that trade was forbidden by Japanese law, that though liable to imprisonment he would be excused on the ground of ignorance and that the only place to apply for special trade privileges was at Nagasaki. A later attempt at contact by one Rezanov in 1804 had a sequel offensive to the Japanese, for two officers under Rezanov's command made raids on Sakhalin and the Kuriles and 'took possession' of these islands in the name of the Czar. This incident must have remained in the minds of the Japanese, for in the nineteenth century the government tried rapidly to fill the empty lands on the island of Hokkaido in order to make certain that Japanese claims to it were perfectly clear. Farmers were given bonuses to encourage them to open up and settle new territory, and thus to forestall any Russian attempts to do the same.

The ambivalent attitude sometimes exhibited by both Russians and Japanese toward each other is well illustrated by the incident of Captain Golownin. This Russian officer, conducting a voyage of exploration in the Pacific in the warship *Diana*, was ordered to investigate the South Kuriles and was captured by a Japanese force in 1811. He was cruelly treated at first, but after nearly two years' imprisonment had so earned the respect and even affection of his guards that they wept when he departed. G. B. Sansom comments that the Japanese attitude to the Russians was 'a mixture of fear and a feeling that perhaps after all they [the Russians] would make good friends'. (*The Western World and Japan*, page 259.) Finally an embassy sent by Czar Nicholas II reached Nagasaki in 1853 and found to their chagrin that Commodore Perry had forestalled them by his negotiations at Uraga Bay. It is doubtful whether the Japanese would have agreed to accept Perry's conditions the next year if the Russians had not already made clear to them over a period their unpreparedness and vulnerability in the face of Western power.

Once the Japanese had joined the military and imperial 'club' of the Western powers, they learned their lesson so well that they inflicted, as has been noted, a severe defeat on the Russians in the war of 1904–5 and began to dissolve the myth of Western invincibility in Asia.

In summary it may thus be said that the Japanese recognise that Russia as a nation poses a threat to their country. Yet Marxist ideas have a strong appeal to Japanese intellectuals. Many of them who are by no means Communist in their leanings tend nevertheless to think in Marxist terms. The governments of the West and particularly of the United States have not as yet taken sufficient account of the appeal of Marxism to Japanese intellectual leaders, an appeal which may well be finding an echo in the minds of leaders in the Third World countries now beginning that development which Japan has already achieved.

## THE CHINESE

The relations of the Japanese and the Chinese cannot be discussed in the same terms as the relations of the Japanese to any other people, for they are distant racial cousins, and have for one another the likes and dislikes common between relatives and near neighbours.

The Japanese acknowledge that they are indebted to China for much of their civilisation at the time of its origins in the early centuries of the Christian era and at intervals thereafter. From China via Korea came written characters, the Buddhist religion, administrative systems, art styles and the beginnings of literature. From about AD 600 to 800 Japan sent embassies to China as part of a deliberate policy to collect information. Until modern times the two nations lived basically at peace with one another. The only serious attempt to invade Japan was Mongol not Chinese in origin. The Japanese made sporadic attacks on the China coast, but these were pirate pinpricks rather than serious invasion attempts.

Beginning in the nineteenth century, Japan put through her programme of modernisation at a greater pace and with greater thoroughness than China. This changed the balance of power and the whole relationship between the two peoples.

Taiwan fell to Japan as a valuable prize in the war of 1894–5. Farther north, first Korea, a traditional Chinese sphere of influence, then Manchuria, a valuable Chinese frontier region, and finally much of north China itself came under the control of the ambitious Japanese Army and provided raw materials and markets for Japanese business. The Japanese military leaders may have calculated in 1937 that they could gain complete control of north China without becoming involved in a war for the whole of China. If that was so, the event proved them wrong, and the weary futility of the long-continued 'China Incident' became an embarrassment to the Japanese Army in spite of their phenomenal successes and their control of the Chinese cities and lines of communication. The expansion of the war to the rest of the Pacific brought ultimate defeat to Japan.

Ironically Japan proved a shelter and training-ground for the early Chinese revolutionaries, such as Sun Yat-sen, whose successors are now changing the balance of power once again in China's favour, in at least the military sense. Politically both countries are now of primary importance on the world scene. Economically Japan is still far ahead of her rival.

Against this turbulent and changing background the visit of Premier Tanaka to Peking in the autumn of 1972 was of great significance. The Japanese acknowledged, in guarded Oriental language, the harm done by their aggression in China, and the visit was hailed by both sides as restoring their relations to 'normal'. It is evident to all, the United States included, that China and Japan need one another and will, where possible, maintain a cooperative relationship in the spheres of trade and technological exchange.

The Japanese are sensitive to the feelings and opinions of other peoples. So far they have maintained what one of their premiers called 'a low posture' in world affairs. But they have now succeeded, beyond their own dreams, in building a modern nation with a strong economic base. They are taking an increasing part in the affairs of other nations through trade, foreign financial aid and technical assistance. They are also travelling widely. It is evident we shall hear much more of the Japanese in the near future. The staff members of the *Asahi* newspaper have just published a book, *The Pacific Rivals*, a series of essays which ran for seven months in a paper with 6 million subscribers. They speak of the American 'curtain of ignorance' about Japan, and mention the possibility of a 'declining America'. Ignorance is not confined to America. It is worth everyone's while to learn more about present-day Japan, and about some of her past which determines much of her present. It is also worth remembering that Japanese understand better than most the value of friendship and the virtue of loyalty.

I

# 9

## *Hints for Visitors*

JAPAN is a formal country, but it is not necessary to be over-awed by this fact. The Japanese are quite aware that foreigners have different conventions. They appreciate in visitors a certain respect for the manners and customs of Japan, not an attempt to copy them exactly—which in any case would be almost impossible. Be yourself—but in a polite way. Sincerity and politeness combined are qualities the Japanese particularly admire.

A good rule on first meeting Japanese people is to behave as you would on the most formal occasion in your own country. You can add to this little touches of what you observe the Japanese doing; but don't overdo it. For example, you should bow slightly but respectfully when they do; but don't attempt to keep up the elaborate series of graded bows some older Japanese execute. They do not expect it of you. On the other hand, it is hardly necessary to add, don't tap shoulders, slap backs, pump hands, hold arms or get familiar in an attempt to be friendly. The Japanese are about twice as formal as the British and four times as formal as Americans.

Do not let me discourage you. With common sense, sincerity and inner friendliness you can safely venture outside the narrow and barren bounds of cosmopolitan hotels and shops into the life of Japan in streets, homes, parks and villages, as and when you get the chance. Keep your distance physically; but your words of real friendship will be deeply and understandingly appreciated, even if they have to be translated.

It is also wise to remember in being polite not to be too

obsequious. The social hierarchy and patronage system obtains strongly in Japan. A businessman of quite moderate rank and wealth can order people about, and is expected to. A prominent surgeon in a hospital is lord of all he surveys, and has subordinates and students do things for him outside the hospital which we would never dream of asking. So if you are a man in some such category travelling in Japan, be courteous, but do not let the strange surroundings deprive you of a sense of your own worth. Japanese will be glad to help you, even serve you. The secret is that they do not think service demeans them.

This brings up the question of introductions. To get anywhere in Japan, in business, in professional work, or even in special shopping or off-the-beaten-track sightseeing, it is most helpful to have at least one or two introductions. The Japanese will do anything for you if they know who you are, if you are a friend of a friend, or even belong to some known and respectable institution with an established identity. There is, of course, a reason for this. Once they admit you to their circle, they are committed to you, for they treat the obligations of family and friendship seriously. So before they start the cycle of giving and receiving favours, they would just like to know you are not going to take advantage of them, that you are in fact the kind of person you say you are.

To make identification easier everyone carries visiting cards, which they produce on all occasions, and hand over formally with two hands, the lettering facing the recipient. Foreigners usually have cards printed with the name of the firm or university on one side in English and on the reverse in Japanese. Have this done ahead of time, or as soon as possible after your arrival, if you are intending to be more than a short-term tourist.

When you have received help or favours from Japanese, whether friends or casual acquaintances, make it a point to thank them. Sometimes a phone call or letter is enough; at other times you will want to give a gift. Be very cautious about giving money; the Japanese have the same feelings as we do about being 'paid' for something, only more so. If cash is clearly in order, as it sometimes is in return for actual cash expended, do not give it as 'naked money' but put it in an envelope. And when you receive a gift, as you will when you least expect it, obviously you will want to give something in return, though not necessarily of exactly the same value. Or send something later from your own country. Craft goods, objects which could not possibly have been made in Japan, are appreciated, if you can find something suitable. It is wise not to admire individual objects in stores too rapturously, if you are with a Japanese friend. You may be embarrassed to find the article delivered to you the next day.

Learning the Japanese language is a life-long task, for its subtleties and involutions, spoken and written, are endless. Japanese is probably one of the most difficult languages on earth, but the first stages are fortunately fairly simple. Most foreigners can acquire in a short time enough everyday Japanese phrases to ask directions, go shopping, order food, and generally get around. The phrase book put out as a complimentary item by Japan Air Lines is excellent for this purpose. At an even simpler level the common phrases of greeting can be learned in an hour. Here are some examples:

| English | Ordinary Japanese phrase | More formal |
| --- | --- | --- |
| Good morning | Ohaiyo gozaimas' | (Women should |
| Good day | Kon nichi wa | always use the |
| Good evening | Kom ban wa | more formal |
| Goodbye | Sayónara (*not* sayonáhra) | phrase, where given) |
| Please | Dozo | |
| Thank you | Arigato | Arigato gozaimas' |
| Thank you very much | | Dom' arigato gozaimas' |
| Excuse me (to get past someone or for casual use) | Gomen nasai | Gomen kudasai |

| English | Ordinary Japanese phrase | More formal |
|---|---|---|
| Excuse me (for a real apology), I am sorry | | Shitsurei itashimas' |
| Hello! (on the telephone) | Moshi, moshi | |
| Welcome! | | Yoku irashaimas' |
| How are you? | Ikaga des' ka | O ikaga de gozaimas' ka |
| Your name? | O namai wa | |
| My name is Watanabe | Watakushi wa Watanabe des' | Watakushi wa Watanabe de gozaimas' |
| I am Watanabe | | |

(Use 'san' after the name for the *other* person, never for yourself. It is a general title meaning Mr, Mrs or Miss.)

| | |
|---|---|
| Where is the toilet? | Te arai wa doko des' ka |
| It's a fine day, isn't it? | Ii otenki des', ne |
| That's enough! (when food is being offered, saké poured) | Mo, takusan |
| Quickly | Hayaku |
| Slowly | Osoku |
| Taxi | Tak(u)si |
| I would like to see that | Sore wo mitai des' |
| How much is this? | Kore wa o ikura des' ka |

| | | | |
|---|---|---|---|
| one | ichi | five | go |
| two | ni | six | roku |
| three | san | seven | shichi |
| four | shi *or* yon | eight | hachi |

| nine   | kyu   | one hundred  | hyaku  |
|--------|-------|--------------|--------|
| ten    | ju    | one thousand | sen    |
| twenty | niju  | ten thousand | man    |
| thirty | sanju |              |        |
| forty  | yonju | half         | hambun |
| etc    |       |              |        |

Japanese is pronounced as it is written. The vowels have approximately the sounds they have in Italian, and stress on each syllable is about equal. Ai and oi are not diphthongs, and an effort should be made to pronounce each vowel separately. This is easy in the second case; Yoichi is pronounced Yo – ee – chee. Double consonants like –tt, –pp are given full value. Pause slightly over them, again as in Italian.

Where s' and m' occur in the above examples, the syllables are usually written su and mo, but the vowels in these cases are almost silent and have therefore here been written with apostrophes.

Now some points about travel and communications. Bright red colour on a telephone does not indicate a hot line, but just a public phone. They work on the same principle as the new ones in Britain; you dial first and put your money in afterwards. When your time is up, the machine makes noises to ask for more money. But come ready with your number written down, for the phone book is very mysterious. Ask a hotel clerk, when you can, to get a number for you. Kobe and Yokohama publish small phone books in English listing the foreign, ie non-Japanese, firms.

Get into the habit of reserving a seat on long-distance trains, for most of them are crowded. On some super-expresses you cannot travel without a reservation (it's all done by computer). Almost all trains run on time. Avoid all subways at rush hour. They pack in twice as many people as can conceivably fit in the space.

The delightful thing about taxis is you don't have to tip the driver. If your destination is in the least obscure, have the address written down, preferably in Japanese, to give to the driver. Japanese addresses go by block numbers, not by street numbers, and are a mystery to the Japanese themselves. In a Japanese taxi as a rule you do not need to open or shut the rear door. The driver does it for you with a lever—courtesy mechanised.

For some the restaurants of Japan will be a gastronomic paradise, for others a confusing maze. Give yourself the full benefit of the infinite variety of eating-places found in the big cities, both Japanese and foreign-style. Some details are given in Chapter 7. Beyond that, ask your Japanese friends for recommendations. Or ask the hotel clerk—he will not take it amiss that you want to eat elsewhere.

After you have overcome the first strangeness of the country, give yourself the opportunity of staying in a Japanese inn. It is a pleasant experience. You may find the remarks in Chapter 3 on how the Japanese live useful in regard to living on the tatami-mat floor, sleeping, eating and so on. A foreign-style breakfast of egg, toast, and coffee or tea, rather than the Japanese fish, rice and seaweed, can be obtained in a Japanese inn. You can also request a back-rest, which makes sitting on the floor much more comfortable. It should no longer be necessary to tell the sophisticated Westerner that no one wears his outdoor shoes in a Japanese house. These are left in the *genkan* or entrance hall, and you step up to the polished wood verandah or matted room in your stocking-soles. Occasionally, as in cold temples, a pair of slippers is provided. And when you go to the toilet, you may find a pair of rubber-soled slippers for use there. You must leave them pointing inwards by stepping out of them backwards when you depart.

Chopsticks are the most civilised of all eating tools. Nearly all the crude cutting up of food with barbaric knives is done in the kitchen. Polite handling of delicate morsels is encouraged by the skilful use of chopsticks. Every visitor should learn to handle them, even though he may also have to employ a spoon to satisfy his hunger.

The following suggestions give a few indications of how a foreigner can amuse himself sightseeing in Japan. But all these places are favourites of the Japanese also. Only a few minimal comments are included, giving an idea as to why they are what the Germans call *Sehenswürdigkeiten* ('things worth seeing'). The reader is referred for all relevant details on season, prices and distances to the excellent guide books and information available from the Japanese National Tourist Organisation, with offices in London, New York and the main cities of Japan, and with many locations at railway stations.

## *Tokyo*
Shopping—many separate areas, but especially the Ginza.
Tokyo Tower.
Imperial Palace—from the outside.
Ueno Park.
Theatres.

## *Environs of Tokyo*
Nikko—Tokugawa temples.
Kegon Waterfall—maples in autumn.
Mt Fuji, Lake Hakone, Izu district, Miyanoshita.
Kamakura.

## *Kyoto*
Kinkakuji—Golden Pavilion Temple, and garden.
Ginkakuji—Silver Pavilion Temple, original tea-ceremony house and gardens.
Kiyomizudera Temple.
Geisha—special parade at New Year time.
Festivals: Yasaka Shrine (New Year)—kimonos worn.
    Cherry Blossom (April).
    Gion Matsuri (July)—floats, and treasures of some houses shown.
    Jidai no Matsuri (Historical Eras Festival, October) —in costume.
Ryoanji—Zen Temple with abstract garden.

*Environs of Kyoto*

Nara—several outstanding temples.

Near Nara—Horyuji Temple, one of the oldest in Japan, with particularly fine images and art objects.

*Other Centres*

Miyajima—Shinto Shrine on Inland Sea, with torii gateway standing in the sea.

Nagasaki—famous for the Mitsubishi Shipyards building giant oil-tankers and for interesting relics of early Portuguese, Dutch and British settlement, Memorial of the Martyrs, and remains of Dutch Island of Deshima.

Atom Bomb Memorial and Museum. Westerners will not want to visit this place, any more than I did. But everyone should. You will meet no resentment from Japanese, but you will have a humbling experience.

The Japanese Alps—in Central Japan. Skiing. Mountain-climbing, with and without guides. Magnificent scenery. Good hotels. Semi-active volcanoes and hot springs.

Hagi—on Sea of Japan coast in south-west of Honshu. Lovely Japanese seaside town, unknown to tourists. Only Japanese inns. Orange groves. Cradle of early reformers in nineteenth century, historically significant.

Hokkaido—Northern island, something different. Scene of Winter Olympics, 1972. Dairy country. Ainu tribal reservations. Can be reached by air, or by train and ferry-boat.

# *Acknowledgements*

This book could not have taken shape without the help of many friends. I owe a debt of gratitude to a friend of many years, Dr Keijiro Suruga of Tokyo and his family, and to Japanese who gave me every facility for research in Nagasaki, Kyoto, Hagi and Mt Koya during January 1971.

A graduate student, now a teacher, Mr Gregory Smith of Seton Hall University, New Jersey, undertook a search for many facts. Dr Carmen Blacker of Cambridge University was kind enough to make some valuable suggestions. The editor and publishers of *Current History* have kindly given permission for material in Chapter 5 to be reproduced from an article which appeared in that journal in April 1971.

No editor could have been more considerate or careful than Miss Evelyn M. Edwards. The Master and Fellows of Clare College, Cambridge, were hospitable to a student who returned after the lapse of years, and the staff of Cambridge University Library gave me every aid.

Finally, the understanding of my wife during the writing of this book has meant much, and to her is due my grateful thanks.

Seton Hall University                                          October 1972
South Orange, New Jersey

# Index